# Study Skills Strategies

*Tips for More Effective Individual, Classroom, and Online Learning*

Third Edition

## Uelaine A. Lengefeld

# *A Crisp Fifty-Minute™ Series Book*

This Fifty-Minute™ Book is designed to be "read with a pencil." It is an excellent workbook for self-study as well as classroom learning. All material is copyright-protected and cannot be duplicated without permission from the publisher. *Therefore, be sure to order a copy for every training participant through our Web site, www.axzopress.com.*

# Study Skills Strategies

*Tips for More Effective Individual, Classroom, and Online Learning*

Third Edition

## Uelaine A. Lengefeld

**CREDITS:**

| | |
|---|---|
| VP, Product Development: | **Adam Wilcox** |
| Editor: | **Marguerite Langlois** |
| Copy Editor: | **Ann Gosch** |
| Production Editor: | **Genevieve McDermott** |
| Production Artists: | **Nicole Phillips, Rich Lehl, Betty Hopkins, and Lisa Delaney** |

**ISBN 10:** 1-4260-9085-4
**ISBN 13:** 978-1-4260-9085-1
Library of Congress Catalog Card Number 2007924816
Printed in the United States of America
3 4 5 09 08

## Learning Objectives for

# STUDY SKILLS STRATEGIES

The learning objectives for *Study Skills Strategies* are listed below. They have been developed to guide the user to the core issues covered in this book.

## The objectives of this book are to help the user:

1) Assess study skills and plan for improvement

2) Practice time-management techniques for successful studying

3) Take clear, meaningful classroom notes and study effectively from them

4) Use the five-step method to develop powerful reading skills

5) Practice memory techniques to enhance ability to learn

6) Improve test performance

7) Develop specific study skills for mathematics and related subjects

## Assessing Progress

A Crisp Series **assessment** is available for this book. The 25-item, multiple-choice and true/false questionnaire allows the reader to evaluate his or her comprehension of the subject matter.

To download the assessment and answer key, go to www.axzopress.com and search on the book title.

*Assessments should not be used in any employee-selection process.*

# About the Author

Uelaine Lengefeld spent more than 40 years as a high school, community college, and university instructor and administrator. She was chairperson of the English department at Claremont High School, honored as the San Gabriel Teacher of the Year, and nominated for State Teacher of the Year. In addition, she taught study skills and coordinated the Educational Opportunity Program (EOP) Instructional Support Center at Cal Poly State University in San Luis Obispo, California.

Later, she was director of the Learning Center and supervisor of the Disabled Students Program at Citrus College in Glendora, California. She also taught English and ESL (English as Second Language) at Citrus. She is now retired from teaching.

Previous editions of *Study Skills Strategies* were translated into Japanese and Spanish and were adapted for use in Great Britain.

# Preface

Fear of the unknown is both normal and healthy. It can be a powerful motivator. On the other hand, too much fear can cause procrastination, and sometimes paralysis. If you learn proven study skills strategies, much of the fear about college, or any new learning experience, will fade.

This book will help you design a study improvement plan based on your skills, needs, and individual situation. Whether you study full-time or part-time, whatever your age, background, or culture, you will find suggestions for tailoring your study plan to give you the best advantage for successful learning.

Your anxiety will diminish and your confidence will grow once you are familiar with the study skills in this book.

You will find that you are able to focus more clearly on important points and organize your note-taking, reading, and review work for more effective learning. This new edition includes tips for using technology to enhance these skills and tips for online learning. You will also find suggestions for getting assistance with any special needs you have.

Achieving all of this will take effort on your part, but if you are serious about your studies, it will be well worth the time you invest.

Your Learning Strategies Coach,

*Uelaine A. Lengefeld*

Uelaine A. Lengefeld

## Acknowledgments

Special thanks go to the late Elwood Chapman for his ideas and for his special mentoring throughout the creation of the first edition. Without Mr. Chapman and the assistance of Lynne Kennedy, the book would never have come to fruition. Michael Crisp's talented editorial pen was essential, and I am grateful for his original assistance.

I also want to acknowledge Professors Walter Lilian Metlitzky, Martha Maxwell, Frank Robinson, Frank Christ, Shuling Cummins, and Colin Rose for research contributions in the field of learning and reading skills.

In this new edition my daughter, Katherine, and her husband, Ray Leung, have been enormously supportive.

Without the help of my daughter and William Argueta and C.J. Desta, members of my daughter's State Farm Insurance staff, this edition would not have been as easily completed.

Also special appreciation goes to Debbie Woodbury for her guidance and to Marguerite Langlois for her insight on new and emerging study issues for today's learners.

## Dedication

With love for Katherine and Ray's children: Gwyneth, angel Max, and Logan.

# Table of Contents

# P A R T 1

# Getting Started

*" To learn is to change. Education is a process that changes the learner."*

**–George B. Leonard, American author**

# Your Attitude Toward Learning

Why did you pick up this book? How do you feel about your study skills? What would you like to change or develop further?

Good study skills are the key to successful learning, and the best way to start improving your skills is to look at where you are now. The assessment on the next two pages is designed to help you know yourself better. This self-assessment is for your personal information. There are no right answers—but for this program to be effective, you must be honest with yourself.

After this assessment, you will find information and ideas on today's diverse classrooms and special needs that students may have, followed by a look at computers as learning tools. You will finish this section with a learning plan to help you set your goals for improving your study skills.

# DISCOVER YOUR ATTITUDE TOWARD LEARNING

To learn and apply quality study skills, it is essential to have a positive attitude. In fact, your attitude and motivation will make all the difference. To measure your attitude toward studying, complete this exercise. If the statement describes your attitude or study habit, check YES and if not check NO. Be very honest.

| Attitudes | Yes | No |
|---|---|---|
| 1. I am satisfied with my test scores on most examinations. | ❏ | ❏ |
| 2. If I do poorly on a test, I increase my efforts and get help from a teacher, a tutor, or a study partner. | ❏ | ❏ |
| 3. When required, I can concentrate on studies. I am not easily distracted. | ❏ | ❏ |
| 4. The challenge of taking study notes on difficult textbook reading does not throw me. | ❏ | ❏ |
| 5. Although busy, I am able to find priority time to study. Procrastination and cramming are not problems for me. | ❏ | ❏ |
| 6. I attend class regularly and carefully prepare for most class sessions. | ❏ | ❏ |
| 7. I have a clear reason for going to school and I know that good study skills will get me closer to my career goal. | ❏ | ❏ |
| 8. When I have a boring instructor, I realize I must work harder to make the material interesting. | ❏ | ❏ |

CONTINUED

| Attitudes | Yes | No |
|---|:---:|:---:|
| 9. My moods or personal problems seldom prevent me from completing my work. | ❏ | ❏ |
| 10. I can visualize myself completing my goal. | ❏ | ❏ |
| 11. I know how to reward myself for finishing a difficult assignment. | ❏ | ❏ |
| 12. I listen carefully while taking class notes, and I review them within 24 hours. | ❏ | ❏ |

The results of this assessment will help you identify areas you need to focus on to improve your study habits. You can use this insight to create a plan to build effective study skills and achieve your learning goals.

# Today's Diverse Classrooms

If you have been in school in recent years, you are already familiar with the diversity represented by today's students. If you have not been in a classroom recently, you may find yourself in an environment more diverse than you have previously experienced.

Diversity creates a rich learning environment where you benefit from the many life experiences of your classmates. You may encounter:

➤ People from various cultures, whose approach to personal development, school, teachers, and study is different from your own

➤ People who speak a variety of languages, who bring different communication patterns represented by their languages

➤ People of many ages learning together, encouraging the sharing of a wide variety of life experiences

➤ People who have various disabilities, who are now able to take part in classrooms in new ways thanks to technology and new types of learning aids

## *Available Help for Specific Needs*

Because of the rapid growth of diversity in classrooms, schools now provide many kinds of assistance for students with special needs. If you are part of any of the groups above, if you are returning to school after several years away from the classroom, or if you have other concerns about studying successfully, take the time to explore and ask for the types of help you would like to have. Speak to a teacher, a counselor, or an adviser.

Here are some examples of what is available:

➤ Study groups and tutoring

➤ ESL (English as Second Language) classes, both as general language classes and as classes for specific study topics

➤ Assistance for students with physical disabilities, including modification of classroom equipment, several types of computer equipment, personal aides, readers, and note-takers

➤ Assistance for those with learning disabilities, including tutoring, study assistance for specific topics, and modification of learning materials and classroom procedures

➤ Career centers to help you choose studies related to your individual work goals and work with any special needs you may have

# WHAT ABOUT YOU?

We each bring our own individual differences and experiences into a classroom. In what ways are you different from other students? Which aspects of diversity do you represent? (It may be something other than the examples given on the preceding page.)

_____

_____

_____

Because of this diversity, what positive contributions can you bring to a group of students? What experience do you have that will enrich your class?

_____

_____

_____

How are you like the other students in your classes? What experiences, ideas, or goals do you share?

_____

_____

_____

What types of help or adaptations might be useful for you in meeting your learning goals?

_____

_____

_____

You may have fears about studying some topics, or about returning to school. This book will help you become a successful student. Think about other skills you have mastered. Learning skills are no different. Some of your skills may need polishing, and you can do this if you are determined to succeed.

# Computers as Learning Tools

Throughout this book, you will find suggestions for using a computer to help you study more effectively. But as you start looking at your approach to studying, it is important to be clear on what a computer can and cannot do for you.

| Computers Can | Computers Cannot |
|---|---|
| Help you take notes more quickly | Ensure your notes will be more accurate |
| Help you file, organize, and store information | Replace thinking about what kind of organization you really need |
| Help you create papers that look organized, neat, and well-formatted | Take away the hard work of creating good content |
| Be a gateway to an enormous amount of information | Replace the need to think carefully about the information you choose and use |

How much you use a computer in the classroom and in your studying depends on several things: what your teacher requires, the specific subject you are studying, what resources you need for the subject, equipment that is available to you, and how comfortable you are with using computers.

Have you been using a computer for years as a learning tool? Then remember that as the topics you study become more advanced, you will need to think more carefully and deeply about what you are learning, and you will need to slow down to do that.

Are you going back to school and not accustomed to regular computer use? Often you will have choices on how much or how little you use your computer as a learning tool. Some people still feel they do better with taking notes by hand while others carry their laptops everywhere. Most teachers today expect that written assignments will be completed on a computer.

You can learn more about computer use in many ways. Talk with your teacher or adviser about what is available at your school. There are also many self-study books you can use; your teacher or adviser can help you choose what works for you.

# Your Focus Points

A definition of *accountability* is to be responsible for one's actions.

We all have good intentions. The thing that separates those who are successful from those who are not is how well these good intentions are carried out.

Creating and putting in writing a specific plan can help convert your good intentions into action. Completing this exercise is a good starting point.

One important study skill is the ability to focus on what is important to you as you learn. Practice this skill now. Answer the following questions to help guide what you learn as you go through this book.

**Note:** It is important for you to work through this entire book. This exercise will help you keep in mind your important focus points.

1. Look back at the assessment you did at the beginning of this part. List below the three things that you most want to focus on as you work through this book.

   _____

   _____

   _____

2. How will your personal culture, background, and experiences help you commit to improving your study skills?

   _____

   _____

   _____

3. Look back at the list you made about the specific needs you have for adaptations and help with learning. How, specifically, will you get those?

   a. List the people you will go to for help with this.

      _____

      _____

   b. When do you plan to do this?

      _____

      _____

If you are working with a tutor, adviser, or someone else to build your study skills, show this plan to that person and ask for his or her ideas.

Now you are ready to continue your work with this book.

# Taking Control of

# Your Time

❝*If you don't know where you are going, you will probably end up somewhere else.*❞

–Dr. Laurence J. Peter, American educator and author

# Make Studying a Priority

Choosing specific times and places for study can be a difficult task, especially if you also have a job, are involved with family, or have other commitments. This section will help you look at where and when you study and give you some tips and strategies for making better use of time and place.

## *A Time—and Place—for Everything*

How much time you spend studying, and where you do it, depends a lot on your individual situation. Which one of these is you? Check (√) or fill in those that apply.

- ❑ I am a full-time student.
- ❑ I am a full-time student, also working part-time.
- ❑ I am a part-time student, also working part-time.
- ❑ I am a part-time student, working full-time.
- ❑ Other_____
- ❑ I have a private place for study.
- ❑ I have a shared space for study.
- ❑ I study wherever and whenever I can grab the chance.
- ❑ Other_____
- ❑ My study schedule will affect other people close to me.
- ❑ I have these other commitments in my life:

_____

_____

_____

_____

How do you balance all the aspects of your life, and give priority to studying? Making clear choices, ranking priorities, and scheduling are the keys. Let's start by looking at time management.

# Say "Yes" to Dedicated Time

Say yes to choices that support your commitment. If you have a choice, you may want to work fewer hours so that you can study more effectively. If you are working full-time and have other major commitments, you may be better off taking fewer courses spread over a longer time.

Say yes to dedicating some time to organize your time and place for study. You can save time later if you spend time doing these things now.

Say yes to talking about your commitment to friends and family. This is especially important if your choices will affect them in any way.

## And Say "No"

You know that you want studying to be a priority. Most people do not have difficulty listing their priorities. The problem is learning when and where to say no.

Learn to say no to extra demands on your time while you are studying. For example, if you are juggling work, study, and family, this may not be a good time to add volunteer work to your life.

Learn to say no to the voice inside your head that says, "I'm too tired to study" or "Let's party." This does not mean school must be a boring or exhausting grind. It simply means that you learn to control your time to ensure there is room for both serious study and relaxation, as well as other priorities in your life.

Learn to say no to multitasking while you are studying. It does not work, and it does not actually save time. You will get more useful studying done if you put aside time for studying and nothing else.

### Think About It

Review the ideas on this page. Which ones are most important for you?

_____

_____

_____

What specific changes will you work on related to these ideas?

_____

_____

_____

# Design a Study Schedule for You

Making choices is essential for academic success. And that applies to how you use your time. The following pages provide time-control tips, techniques, and strategies. By following these time-management tips, you will be able to design your own flexible study schedule.

It is a good idea to follow your study schedule carefully for two or three weeks (making minor adjustments as needed) until it becomes routine. Remember, not all habits are bad; there are *good* habits too!

The exercises on the following pages encourage you to:

➤ Set up calendars and schedules for yourself

➤ Keep them where they are clearly visible

➤ Keep them where you can work with them easily

You can set up a study schedule on your computer, you can choose one of the many planning calendars or diaries that are available to buy, or you can create your own on paper, whichever works best for you.

*Tip:* *If you do set them up on your computer, be sure you have a disk or paper backup.*

Begin with the assessment that starts on the next page.

# HOW WELL ARE YOU USING YOUR TIME?

| If you answer NO to any of these questions, set a date to get started on those items. | YES | NO | Date to Start |
|---|:---:|:---:|:---:|
| **1. Do you have a large monthly calendar?**<br><br>Write all important tests, deadlines, and activities on a large monthly calendar. Place it in a conspicuous location. Use color to highlight important dates or events (like exams). | ❑ | ❑ | _____ |
| **2. Do you have a weekly appointment calendar?**<br><br>Use one that shows a "week at a glance" and has space for daily scheduling, so you have a good overview of the entire week. | ❑ | ❑ | _____ |
| **3. Do you have a weekly study plan?**<br><br>Use a weekly study schedule to visualize and organize your time. Lightly pencil in your classes (by title on the days and times they meet) and block out times to eat, sleep, work, study, and relax. | ❑ | ❑ | _____ |

CONTINUED

CONTINUED

| If you answer NO to any of these questions, set a date to get started on those items. | YES | NO | Date to Start |
|---|---|---|---|
| **4. Do you plan for at least one hour of study for each class period?**<br><br>Protect time each day for study. With a regular schedule, your study time will soon become habit forming. | ❑ | ❑ | _____ |
| **5. Do you plan for study breaks?**<br><br>Remember to limit your straight study time to no longer than one hour. It is important to take a 10-minute break between study periods to refresh yourself and give your mind a rest. | ❑ | ❑ | _____ |
| **6. Do you preview text assignments and review classroom notes from the previous class before your study time?**<br><br>Build this strategy into your weekly schedule. Note time for preview and review on your schedule. | ❑ | ❑ | _____ |
| **7. Do you make effective use of any commute time to school each day (sometimes called dead time)?**<br><br>If you travel to class and have an opportunity to do some schoolwork, this is an ideal time to preview or review. Mark all commute time on your schedule. | ❑ | ❑ | _____ |

CONTINUED

CONTINUED

| If you answer NO to any of these questions, set a date to get started on those items. | YES | NO | Date to Start |
|---|:---:|:---:|:---:|
| **8. Do you leave sufficient time for relaxation and play?**<br><br>Play is therapeutic. Without it you are only half a person. Make sure you have time for play noted on your calendar. You might also want to include relaxing activities such as exercise and meditation. | ❑ | ❑ | _____ |
| **9. Do you reward yourself for meeting goals?**<br><br>Find small treats that are affordable or even free. (Do not accept your reward if you do not meet your goal!) | ❑ | ❑ | _____ |
| **10. Are you a list maker?**<br><br>It is a great idea to keep lists. Assign a priority to items on your list and complete the most important ones first. Carry forward items not completed to your next list. | ❑ | ❑ | _____ |

Here is a chance to practice setting priorities for yourself. As you did this assessment, you probably noted several things you want to do or improve. Write your three top priorities, and the dates you have chosen to start working on them, here:

First priority _____ Date to start _____

Second priority _____ Date to start _____

Third priority_____ Date to start _____

# Choose What Is Most Important

Setting priorities and writing them down is an important practice for good time management. If you do not already do this, start now. You can use the format here, or any other format that works for you. This kind of list-making should become a habit.

If you already do this regularly, take a minute to think about it: Does your system work for you? If not, use the sample on the next page to play with new ideas for yourself.

If you are not in the habit of ranking priorities, take a few minutes now to practice on the next page, listing your priorities for today (or tomorrow). Use the letters A, B, or C to note which ones are most important (the letter A representing the most important).

As you work on your priorities, remember that setting priorities means making choices, not trying to fit everything in. Make choices that say yes to some things, and no to others.

*Tip:* *Be realistic. Plan to accomplish a few projects or errands each day. As you complete an item, check it off. You may need to change your expectations to increase your performance.*

# TODAY'S PRIORITY LIST

Date: _____

| Priority<br>A, B, or C | School | Done |
|:---:|:---|:---:|
| _____ | 1. _____ | ❑ |
| _____ | 2. _____ | ❑ |
| _____ | 3. _____ | ❑ |
| _____ | 4. _____ | ❑ |
| _____ | 5. _____ | ❑ |

**Work**

| | | |
|:---:|:---|:---:|
| _____ | 1. _____ | ❑ |
| _____ | 2. _____ | ❑ |
| _____ | 3. _____ | ❑ |
| _____ | 4. _____ | ❑ |
| _____ | 5. _____ | ❑ |

**Personal**

| | | |
|:---:|:---|:---:|
| _____ | 1. _____ | ❑ |
| _____ | 2. _____ | ❑ |
| _____ | 3. _____ | ❑ |
| _____ | 4. _____ | ❑ |
| _____ | 5. _____ | ❑ |

# Weekly Scheduling

The time-use assessment you completed earlier included several ideas on weekly scheduling. Time for study, work, play, relaxation, and other commitments are all important to include each week. This schedule is an important tool for balancing all aspects of your life. The example on the next page shows a weekly schedule for someone who studies part-time and works part-time.

## *Example of a Weekly Study Schedule*

|  |  | MON | TUES | WED | THU | FRI | SAT | SUN |
|---|---|---|---|---|---|---|---|---|
| **AM** | 6–7 | ←———————Breakfast——————→ | | | | | | |
| | 7–8 | Get Ready for School Review | | | | | | |
| | 8–9 | History | Chem. | History | Chem. | History | | |
| | 9–10 | Study | | Study | | Study | | |
| | 10–11 | | Study | | Study | | | |
| | 11–12 | English | | English | | English | | |
| **PM** | 12–1 | ←——————————Lunch——————————→ | | | | | | |
| | 1–2 | Work | Work | Work | Work | Work | Work | Study |
| | 2–3 | | | | | | | |
| | 3–4 | | | | | | | |
| | 4–5 | | | | | | | |
| | 5–6 | Study | Gym | Study | Gym | | | |
| | 6–7 | ←——————————Dinner——————————→ | | | | | | |
| | 7–8 | Study | Study | Study | Study | | | Study |
| | 8–9 | | | | | | | |
| | 9–10 | | | | | | | |

Now turn to the blank weekly schedule on the next page and write in what would be a realistic schedule for you.

***Tip:*** *Do this in pencil! You may want to change it again as you work on it, or as you go through this book.*

After you have an idea of the kind of schedule that works for you, you can put it or something similar in whatever paper or computer form works best for you.

# WEEKLY SCHEDULE

|  |  | MON | TUES | WED | THU | FRI | SAT | SUN |
|---|---|---|---|---|---|---|---|---|
| **AM** | 6–7 |  |  |  |  |  |  |  |
|  | 7–8 |  |  |  |  |  |  |  |
|  | 8–9 |  |  |  |  |  |  |  |
|  | 9–10 |  |  |  |  |  |  |  |
|  | 10–11 |  |  |  |  |  |  |  |
|  | 11–12 |  |  |  |  |  |  |  |
| **PM** | 12–1 |  |  |  |  |  |  |  |
|  | 1–2 |  |  |  |  |  |  |  |
|  | 2–3 |  |  |  |  |  |  |  |
|  | 3–4 |  |  |  |  |  |  |  |
|  | 4–5 |  |  |  |  |  |  |  |
|  | 5–6 |  |  |  |  |  |  |  |
|  | 6–7 |  |  |  |  |  |  |  |
|  | 7–8 |  |  |  |  |  |  |  |
|  | 8–9 |  |  |  |  |  |  |  |
|  | 9–10 |  |  |  |  |  |  |  |

1. When do you plan for the next day or week? _____

2. When do you review your notes for the previous week? _____

3. How many times a week do you review the text or notes for a class? _____

4. Do you record lectures (with the instructor's permission) and listen during your commute or when you are completing routine tasks?_____

# Your Study Space

Where you study is just as important as when you study. Using the right study space means that you can concentrate and do better work. Often, it also means that you can work longer than if you are in a distracting or uncomfortable place. You can create a useful study space for yourself even if you share that space with someone else.

You can also take advantage of different places that may be available to you during the day, such as a library, or while you are waiting for an appointment.

Make a practice of carrying at least one study item wherever you go—a book, notes, or a laptop—so that you can use them any time for short periods of study. But save your more difficult reading and assignments for when you have the best study spaces.

Give special attention to the place you use most often to study and make it work for you.

## Think About It

Answer the following questions. Use them to help you decide what you need to make your study space work better for you.

1. Do you have a private study space, such as your own room? Or do you share a space with someone else?

   _____

   _____

   _____

2. What kind of lighting does your study space have? Could you improve it? How?

   _____

   _____

   _____

3. Do you have plenty of space for your books, computer, and other study materials? Could you improve this space? How?

   _____

   _____

   _____

4. Do you have a chair and a writing space that helps you maintain good posture while you work? Could you improve that? How?

   _____

   _____

   _____

5. When you study away from your regular study space, do you choose spaces that allow you to concentrate well, if possible? What kinds of spaces might work better for you?

   _____

   _____

   _____

# Time Control: It's Your Choice!

Here is a summary of the time-control tips in this section. Good time control is about making choices that work for you. Review these tips and check (√) those that are most important for you to practice.

❑ Keep a written list of your priorities and review them regularly for needed changes.

❑ Create a schedule that supports your commitment to learning.

❑ Create a schedule that shows a realistic balance in your life.

❑ Talk with friends and family about your study needs and commitment.

❑ Create a monthly schedule that shows all major activities for the month.

❑ Create a weekly schedule that shows specific times for study and other activities.

❑ Look for added opportunities to study, such as commute times or between classes.

❑ Plan for preview and review times before and after classes.

❑ Arrange the place where you do most of your study so that it is well-lit, comfortable, and stocked with the resources and equipment you need.

❑ Reward yourself when you meet your goals.

# Note-Taking

# Techniques

*There is no such thing as a worthless conversation, providing you know what to listen for. And questions are the breath of life for a conversation."*

**–James Nathan Miller, writer**

# Prepare for Effective Note-Taking

Note-taking is one of the most important things you do in class. It is your first step in working with the class material. When you take notes well, you are on your way to mastering the important information from each class.

Taking good notes starts with the way you approach the class. Here are some tips for preparing yourself:

1. Always read your assignment before you come to class. This will give you background information and make the lecture easier to understand. Be prepared!

2. Find a seat near the front of the room. Up close, you can see visual aids, be more aware of the instructor's facial expressions, hear better, and be less inclined to daydream.

3. Identify other serious students in each class and get to know them. Get their phone numbers in case you have questions or need help during the term.

4. Learn to listen for main ideas. Abbreviate when possible. Do not try to write down everything the instructor says.

5. Learn to watch the instructor and copy everything he or she writes. This is especially true for examples, solutions, outlines, and definitions.

6. Organize and index your notes in a way that works for you. If you are allowed to use the notes on any exam, you will be ahead of the game.

7. If you have difficulty taking notes because of any limitations you have, talk with your instructor or adviser. Most schools have assistance available or can help you find the resources you need.

The tips outlined on the next few pages will give you specific ideas on taking notes that work for you.

# Choose a Note-Taking Format

There is more than one way to take notes effectively, beginning with choosing whether to write notes on paper or to use a computer. Then you can decide if you prefer to jot down important points informally or to structure your notes in a more formal outline style. The sample notes on the pages that follow will illustrate these variations.

***Tip:*** *The guidelines on this page are presented in outline format to refresh your memory on how to outline material. As you read, check (√) or highlight the tips that are important for you.*

I. **Choose and prepare your tools**

    A. If you use paper, keep your notes organized in a spiral or three-hole notebook.

        1. Avoid loose-leaf folders that allow pages to get lost.

        2. Don't forget extra pens or pencils!

    B. If you use a laptop, have software and folders set up so that you can start taking notes immediately in class.

II. **Set up your format**

    A. Review the sample notes that follow. Use one of these formats or experiment with something similar until you have a format you like.

    B. Date each lecture and number all pages for that course in sequence.

    C. Write recall words and abbreviations of main ideas in a margin or other specific place.

        1. Fill in recall words when you first review your notes.

        2. Leave room to write study questions on the same page or a facing page to assist you when you review.

    D. In your own words, summarize the main ideas in a specific place on the page (or write questions you need to ask your instructor).

    E. Use an outline rather than writing full paragraphs.

        1. Indent secondary ideas, supporting documentation, or examples.

        2. Always leave room when a new point is being developed.

        3. Use incomplete sentences or phrases. (Notice the phrases used on the samples.) Make sure you know the meaning of all your incomplete sentences.

# Structured Note-Taking

This style organizes key ideas in outline form on the right-hand page and study notes on the left-hand page. It is clear and simple to read. Its value is in stressing key points and important words that you can use later as a guide for more detailed study, perhaps from a textbook. Notice the space reserved for vocabulary or other information.

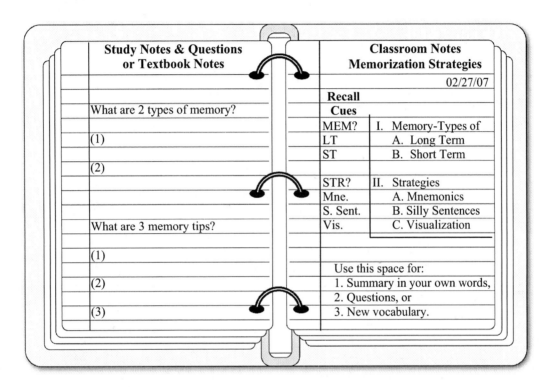

| Study Notes & Questions or Textbook Notes | Classroom Notes Memorization Strategies |
|---|---|

**Left page — Study Notes & Questions or Textbook Notes:**

What are 2 types of memory?

(1)

(2)

What are 3 memory tips?

(1)

(2)

(3)

**Right page — Classroom Notes Memorization Strategies — 02/27/07:**

Recall Cues

| Recall Cues | Outline |
|---|---|
| MEM? | I. Memory-Types of |
| LT |   A. Long Term |
| ST |   B. Short Term |
| STR? | II. Strategies |
| Mne. |   A. Mnemonics |
| S. Sent. |   B. Silly Sentences |
| Vis. |   C. Visualization |

Use this space for:
1. Summary in your own words,
2. Questions, or
3. New vocabulary.

## Think About It

Compare this format to your own approach to note-taking.

Which note-taking ideas in this format might be helpful to you?

_____

_____

Some formats are better for specific class subjects. Would this type of format be useful for any subjects you are studying or plan to study? Which ones?

_____

_____

# Informal Note-Taking

This format uses a different, less-formal kind of outline. Notice that although the notes may look less formal, they are still well-organized. Organization is key no matter what your preferred style. Notice that the student in this example has made additional notes on studying and on what the teacher has stressed as important.

TOPIC: MEMORIZATION                    Sept 27

TWO TYPES OF MEM — difference
important!
    Long term
    Short term
Check text for diff uses of each kind

MEM STRATEGIES (look up words in text)
    Mnemonics — uses first letters
    Silly sentences — fun to use
    Visualization — see it any way that helps

Remember TEST on this chapter on Friday!
Vocabulary and examples imp!

## Think About It

Compare this format to your own approach to note-taking.

Which note-taking ideas in this format might be helpful to you?

_____

_____

Some formats are better for specific class subjects. Would this type of format be useful for any subjects you are studying or plan to study? Which ones?

_____

_____

# Note-Taking by Computer

This example shows notes taken on a laptop. When taking notes on a computer, you could use a format similar to the two previous ones. Notice that this student has kept formatting simple; using fancy fonts or formats would only waste time. You can, however, take advantage of electronic features such as underlining, bold, and highlighting if you are comfortable using them quickly during a lecture. You can also set up organized folders and documents for each subject.

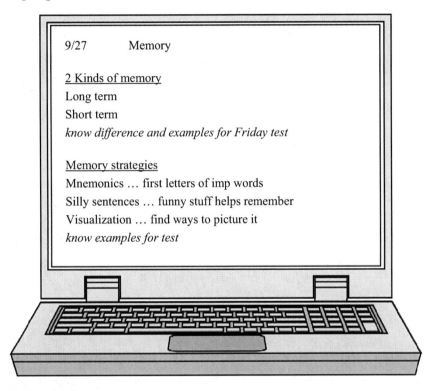

9/27          Memory

<u>2 Kinds of memory</u>
Long term
Short term
*know difference and examples for Friday test*

<u>Memory strategies</u>
Mnemonics … first letters of imp words
Silly sentences … funny stuff helps remember
Visualization … find ways to picture it
*know examples for test*

## Think About It

Compare this format to your own approach to note-taking.

Which note-taking ideas in this format might be helpful to you?

_____

_____

Some formats are better for specific class subjects. Would this type of format be useful for any subjects you are studying or plan to study? Which ones?

_____

_____

# The Keys: Listening and Participation

Setting up your note-taking format is only the first step. After that comes the real work: focusing and getting all the important ideas and details. Listening and participation are your keys to effective note-taking and learning.

**I.  Listening**

  A.  Stay focused on the teacher and listen for key ideas.

  B.  Listen for the following signals from your instructor about what is important:

   1.  Voice changes usually indicate important points—listen for increases in volume or dramatic pauses.

   2.  Repetition is a clue that an important point is being made.

   3.  Gestures may indicate a major point.

  C.  Listen to and stay involved in all classroom discussions.

  D.  Ask questions, especially when things are unclear.

**II.  Taking Lecture Notes**

  A.  What points should you note?

   1.  Key ideas and main points

   2.  All important terms and definitions

   3.  Lists

   4.  Formulas or solutions

  B.  Listen for secondary ideas. Indent or space so you can see they are secondary.

  C.  Listen for connections and draw arrows to show connections between ideas.

  D.  Whenever you are in doubt, write it down. In discussion classes, jot notes on important points—particularly questions asked and conclusions reached during the discussion.

  E.  Spell new words as well as you can by the sound. Look up correct spelling the first chance you get, or ask your instructor for help.

  F.  Use symbols, diagrams, or drawings to illustrate ideas.

### III. Participate in Class

    A. Think, react, reflect, and question to help your instructor keep the class lively.

    B. Become involved but do not grandstand or dominate the conversation.

    C. Your grade will often improve as you actively participate. If you are on the borderline between grades, most instructors will remember your desire to learn if you participate.

# WHAT DO YOU NEED TO PRACTICE?

Use the outline below to focus on what you need to do to improve your note-taking skills. Under each topic, use the A and B lines to write what you most need to change or practice when you take notes. Use the information you have just read to give you ideas.

I. Listening – What I need to practice or change:

    A. _____

    B. _____

II. Taking lecture notes – What I need to practice or change:

    A. _____

    B. _____

III. Class participation – What I need to practice or change:

    A. _____

    B. _____

# Different Notes for Different Needs

You will take better notes and get more out of your classes if you learn to adjust your note-taking to the type of class and the subject. Some classes are based on discussion of ideas, while others are based on facts and definitions. Your teacher may be using lecture, discussion, visual aids, lab work, or any combination of these. Here are some added tips for taking notes in different situations.

As you read, place a check (√) near the tips that are important for you.

❑ When there is a lot of discussion in the class, note the questions and ideas that your classmates bring up, whether you agree with them or not. Note also the further questions and conclusions the teacher emphasizes.

❑ In a lab class, note the topic and the reason for the lab work. Note all the steps you take in the work, and if you have choices, why you picked the choices you made. Note any conclusions you come to, or any results.

❑ When the teacher uses various visual aids—from simple charts and posters to PowerPoint presentations or videos—note what points the teacher emphasizes with the visual aid. Take notes on all the key points that are illustrated. Ask if the visual aid—such as PowerPoint slides or a video—will be available for study later.

❑ When the class involves a lot of factual, specific information—for example, a science or math class—note as much of the information as you can during the class. Add definitions or examples during the class, or note where you can get them later.

❑ Use your textbooks for added note-taking, whether you use them during the class period or not. Highlight and underline. Make notes in the margins. Use the table of contents and the index to help you find information.

❑ When you take an online class, you still need to take notes. As in any other class, use your notes to focus on main topics, important details, and organization of ideas to help you study.

❑ If you have special needs related to note-taking, ask your teacher or adviser to help you with the adaptations or assistance you need.

# Improve Your Note-Taking Speed

Whether you take notes by hand or use a computer, it helps to be able to note things quickly. Note-taking is not the time for anything fancy or elaborate. Your goal is to get the information down.

## Taking Notes by Hand

You can increase your writing speed by changing your handwriting.

➤ Write a sentence in your normal handwriting in the space below.

_____

_____

➤ Observe the writing samples below that have excessive details. Now look at your sample (above) does it have any excessive strokes or flourishes? Notice how difficult they are to decipher.

*Note-taking is not the time for fancy writing.*

➤ Simplify your handwriting; some printing may be necessary.

*Note-taking is the time to simplify. Change ∫ to I.*

## Taking Notes Using a Computer

Use only one easy-to-read font, in a point size of at least 11 or 12, so you can clearly see what is on your screen as you type.

Leave spell-checking for later, except for important words related to the lesson.

If you would like to improve or speed up your keyboarding, a number of programs are available.[1] Check your school bookstore or your favorite office-supply or computer store.

## Review Immediately!

Whenever possible, spend five to 20 minutes reviewing your notes immediately after class, or as soon as you can. Fill in missing areas and rewrite garbled notes. Studies show that short periods of study improve long-term memory.

---

[1] For an excellent book on learning to type using the touch-typing method, see *KAZ® (Keyboarding A-Z)*, a Crisp Series book by Thomson Learning.

## *Use Note-Taking Abbreviations*

Abbreviate, omit, invent, and simplify in any way that helps you. Just remember that you will have to read and understand the notes afterward! Be sure that you use abbreviations that work for you.

| EXAMPLES OF NOTE-TAKING ABBREVIATIONS | | | |
|---|---|---|---|
| > | increase | = | equals |
| < | decrease | ex. | example |
| → | caused, led to | def. | definition |
| w/ w/o | with, without | i.e. | that is |
| ≠ | unequal | vs. | versus |
| sig. | significant | bec. | because |
| imp. | Important | esp. | especially |

## *Text-Messaging Abbreviations*

Text messaging has created a new way of abbreviating words—for example, using IC for "I see," RU for "Are you?" or 4U for "for you." If you are familiar with text-messaging language, then put it to work for you when you take notes, whether you take notes by hand or on your laptop. Text messaging is designed to put as much information as possible in as few characters as possible, so it is ideal for note-taking.[1]

### Think About It

Do you use other types of abbreviations? Add your own below:

_____

_____

_____

---

[1] To learn more about text message abbreviations, read *Fat-Free Writing* by Carol Andrus, a Crisp Series book by Thomson Learning.

# Taking Research Notes

When you are doing research as added study, or as part of writing a presentation or a paper, use the same skills as for taking class notes. Pay attention to main points, look for subordinate ideas, and organize your notes so you can use them later.

Take and sort your notes by topic. If you just write bits of information one after another on the same page, you will have a lot of hard work ahead of you when you start using those notes. Use a method that allows you to separate notes by topic as you go along.

## *Improve Your Research Skills*

Whether you use a library, search online, or find other resources, learn how to focus your research so you can get what you need without wasting a lot of time. Jot down ahead of time your general subject and some of the specifics you might be looking for.

Librarians can help you get started and show you how to use the library's resources. Most libraries now have online catalogs, so you can look for material you might want to use even before you go to the library. Some schools have classes on how to do research; take advantage of them if you can.

For doing research online, learn to do specific and advanced searches. Most search engines have directions for this. Otherwise, you will be faced with far more information than you could ever use. Also, be sure that any information you find is accurately related to what you are doing. Similar words and phrases can bring up Web sites that look like what you want but are not actually related to your topic.

## *Taking Research Notes by Hand*

If you take research notes by hand, the tried-and-true method of using index cards—one card for each item of information—is still the best way to go. Each time you find information you can use, write it on a card.

At the top of the card, write the topic it relates to. Below the information, write where you got it: the author, the book or publication, the page number, the publisher, the date of publication, and any other important publication information.

When you are ready to start writing, it is easy to sort out your cards by topic and line them up the way you will use the information in your work.

## *Taking Research Notes by Computer*

Look back at the ideas above for taking notes by hand. You want to accomplish the same thing—notes that are separate and easy to sort by topic. You also want to have the same information: notes, topic, source. Some software programs have note features that simulate separate index cards. You can also do something like this with any word processing program: set up a separate page for each topic, and put all the information that relates to that topic on the page that you have set up for it.

When you are ready to start writing, you can easily organize your notes further using the features that allow you to move text around.

## *Your Notes Are Not Your Paper*

Always—*always!*—write your own paper or presentation from your notes and research sources. Your notes are just the beginning. They are the information you will use to create your own work; they are support for your work.

Always—*always!*—credit your sources. Tempting as it is, especially with the ease of finding information on the Internet and creating cut-and-paste documents on a computer, never use someone else's work and pass it off as your own. Follow the instructions your teacher gives you for noting sources as you write your paper.

# Review and Focus

Here are the key points and tips for note-taking covered in this section. Use the lines at the bottom of the page to write those that you want to focus on as you develop your study skills.

➤ Prepare yourself for each class by doing assignments and reading before the class.

➤ Use note-taking tools that work for you: notebooks, binders, or your computer.

➤ Set up a system for note-taking. Include the date, the topic, and an organized way of setting up your notes on the page.

➤ In class, listen for main ideas, subtopics, and all important facts.

➤ Take an active part in class. It will help you learn more, and it will help you pay attention for good note-taking.

➤ Use handwriting or keyboarding techniques that allow you to take notes quickly.

➤ Adapt your note-taking to the kind of class you are in. Different subjects and different kinds of classes require specific kinds of notes.

➤ Request help with various types of adaptations if you need them.

➤ Review your notes as soon as possible after class to fill in any added information or to rewrite something that is not clear.

➤ When you take notes for research, set up your notes so that you can easily sort and organize them.

➤ When you take notes for research, include the information, the topic, and the source.

➤ Always credit your sources when you use information or work from someone else.

Write here the points that you want to focus on to develop your note-taking skills:

_____

_____

_____

_____

_____

# Critical Reading

# Skills

> *Language is the soul of the intellect, and reading is the essential process by which that intellect is cultivated beyond the commonplace experiences of everyday life."*

—**Charles Scribner Jr., publisher**

# Reading: Your Key to Better Learning

Effective reading is probably the most important element of becoming an excellent student. If you can read well, you will:

- Get more out of your classes and your textbooks
- Be able to complete your reading assignments more easily
- Understand more clearly what you read
- Be able to pick out the essential information you need for assignments or research

With strong reading skills, you can help yourself learn. Unfortunately, not everyone is gifted with good reading ability. Like any other skill, however, reading can be developed and improved with practice.

## *Five Steps to Better Reading*

In the pages ahead, you will learn a five-step reading strategy that will help you improve your reading skills. The strategy is called SQ3R. The five steps of this strategy will show you how to become a more critical reader—how to think carefully while you read.

You will find that whether you are taking notes, attending class, or reading, your goals are similar. You want to focus on the main ideas, sort out the subtopics, and find the important details.

## *Do You Need Extra Help?*

For many reasons, some people need extra help with reading skills. Perhaps English is your second language. Or maybe you know that you have never really learned to read in any kind of detail, and you feel that you just barely get by with basic reading. You are not alone—many people need some added help with reading, and that is why schools and libraries have all kinds of help available. Talk with your teacher, your adviser, or a librarian. Do not be afraid to ask. By getting help, you are showing how much learning means to you.

# SQ3R for Success

When you read a novel you like, you can move right along enjoying yourself. When you read a love letter, you savor each word and have absolutely no difficulty concentrating. You do not need to underline the main ideas or make marginal notes.

Textbook reading is different. You must learn to apply special reading and marking skills when you study complicated materials. An expansion of the SQ3R reading technique (explained below) can reduce your study time and significantly increase your ability to grasp essential information.

## *Overview of SQ3R*

The name SQ3R will help you remember the five steps in the process:

**Step 1:** Survey

**Step 2:** Question

**Step 3:** Read—and underline

**Step 4:** Recite—and write

**Step 5:** Review

If you have already learned this process, it may not have included underlining and writing in Steps 3 and 4. They are added here because they are important when you are reading to learn something specific.

### Reading Material Online

If you read material online, use the same process. Take notes by hand as you read—you will probably not be able to highlight, underline, or write notes in the margin of the material. Use the five steps to guide your notes.

# SQ3R Step 1: Survey

Spend no more than 10 minutes to survey what you are going to read. This is like taking a "sneak preview" of the reading you have been assigned. You may not be in the habit of previewing and will have to consciously force this important first step.

## *Surveying for an Overview*

Previewing provides an overview of the way the book, chapter, or reading assignment is organized. Smart travelers use a road map and smart students survey first. You are making your own road map to follow as you read.

When you survey, do the following:

➤ Examine the title of each chapter.

➤ Note headings and subheadings and the relationship between the important headings in each chapter.

➤ Glance at diagrams, graphs, or visuals.

➤ Quickly skim the introductory and concluding sections of each chapter.

➤ Notice any study questions or activities at the end of the chapter.

If you are reading online, make some quick notes for yourself as you survey.

As you read this book, you can see how this works. Take a minute or two to turn ahead and skim through the next part. Look at the headings and subheadings. Glance at the exercises. Do not read—just survey to see what the part is about.

After you have surveyed what you are going to read, you are ready to move on to the next step.

# SQ3R Step 2: Question

Your next step is to see each part of what you read as the answer to a question. These questions will help you focus on what is important. For example, the first page of this section focuses on three questions:

➤ Why are reading skills important for learning?

➤ What is SQ3R?

➤ How do you get help with reading if you need it?

When you question, you help yourself understand more of what you are reading, and you prepare yourself to focus on and remember the important points.

Begin with the first section of a chapter. Always read with the intent to answer a question. Use the words who, what, when, where, why, or how to help you turn each heading into a question.

If you are reading online, write down the questions you use.

# PRACTICE

See if you can do this with what you have just read for Step 1 and Step 2 of SQ3R:

Two questions for Step 1:

   1 _____

   2. _____

Two questions for Step 2:

   1. _____

   2. _____

*Compare your answers with the author's suggestions in the Appendix.*

# SQ3R Step 3: Read and Underline

Read each section with the question you developed in mind. *After* reading the section, go back to the beginning and underline, highlight, or mark the material using the techniques on this page and the next.

Read carefully and take your time. Speed reading techniques should not be used for technical material because important details may be missed. Do not be afraid to move your lips or read aloud. It is a myth that rereading a sentence is harmful. Critical reading may require you to reread items several times to completely understand a sentence or passage.

*Tip:* *Use a pen instead of a pencil, because pencil fades. If you prefer, use a highlighter. You could apply different colors for different kinds of information.*

If you read online, you can mark items if the software or program you are using allows you to do that. If it does not, make brief written notes on paper for yourself as you go along.

## Suggestions for Marking

There are a lot of ways to mark what you read. Study these suggestions and adapt them so that they work for you.

### A. Underline after reading

Read a paragraph or a section of the text and then go back and underline only the main points. Do not underline the first time you read the material. When you first read, read for understanding, not trying to memorize at that time.

### B. Use Numbers

Write numbers to help you focus on a series of details.

Use numbers for:     1) lists

                        2) enumerations

                        3) sequences

### C. Vertical Line

Place vertical lines in the margin, like the line you see here, to emphasize main points that include several lines of text.

### D. Asterisks

Use asterisks to signal *main points* and for other important points or ideas.

### E. Recall Phrases

Place recall phrases in the margin to condense major points and provide supporting details. Summaries and questions may also be placed in the margin.

### F. Definitions and Examples

Underline all definitions. Write "def" in the margin. Put parentheses ( ) around examples. If you underline or highlight the entire example, nothing will stand out and your purpose for marking will be lost.

### G. Circles or Boxes

Some students like to (circle) important concepts, ideas, or subheadings.

Other students prefer a box.

### H. Highlighting

Highlight the points underlined or highlight instead of underlining. Use a felt-tip pen. Yellow is often preferred. For online reading, some software programs include a highlighting feature.

### I. ??!!

React to what you read. Agree, disagree! Question? Stay involved with the ideas in the text! Show your reactions with any kind of punctuation or other mark that works for you.

## PRACTICE

As with any skill, practice is the best way to learn marking skills. Would you be confident that you could drive a car after simply listening to a lecture?

You may also want to show your instructor a sample of your markings until you are confident you are selecting the most important material in each paragraph. If suggested, take a reading class and continue to learn new vocabulary words, even after you graduate.[1]

Read the paragraphs in the box on the next page. Then underline or highlight and add recall phrases in the left margin. Apply other marking techniques in a way that works for you.

CONTINUED

---

[1] To learn more about improving your vocabulary, read *Vocabulary Improvement*, a Crisp Series book by Thomson Learning.

## ACADEMIC PRESSURE

Of course academic pressure is not applied evenly during the semester or quarter. There are times (especially during midterms and finals) when all your professors will expect special work from you at once. Themes will be due and examinations will be scheduled all within a few days. These demanding periods produce unusual pressure and strain, especially if you have made the mistake of getting behind in your work. The pace picks up, frustrations increase, fear takes a firmer grip, and students appear haggard and drained. It's a period of too much coffee, too many pills, and too little sleep—a desperate time with a touch of madness. Not only does it hurt your physical and mental health, but when the pressures force abnormal behavior, you can make foolish mistakes and jeopardize your academic progress.

How can you protect yourself from this peak period madness? How can you avoid becoming too tense and frantic? Here are three suggestions: Stick as close as possible to your regular study and work schedule. Avoid late hours. Get some extra work done, but get enough sleep to avoid the tension merry-go-round that spins some students into a state of chaos. Avoid stimulants. Stay away from excessive coffee and drugs that keep you awake but destroy your ability to think clearly and logically when you need to. Assume an air of detachment from the whole crazy rat race. Look at it from a distance. Float through it with a calm head and confident manner. Watch the behavior of others who fall prey to the pressures, but refuse to become over involved yourself. But what if the pressure builds up too much despite your preventive measures? Is there a last-minute safety valve? Physical exercise is a good antidote. Jog. Play ball. Go bowling. Physical activity is one way to reduce stress resulting from a heavier-than-usual academic load.

Reprinted with the permission of the author, Elwood N. Chapman, *College Survival: A Do-It-Yourself Guide.*

*Compare your markings with the author's suggestions in the Appendix.*

# SQ3R Step 4: Recite and Write

Once you have formed questions on your reading and have read to answer those questions, you are ready to recite the answers. Use your underlining and markings to guide you. Reciting helps you learn and remember what you have read. Do not skip this step, even if you think you know the information. This step will make a big difference in how well you master the material.

Recite the answers out loud (or quietly to yourself). Also write brief study notes, which will help encode the information in your long-term memory for easier retrieval on the final examination.

Write a sentence summary of the main idea in each paragraph if the material is extremely difficult for you.

The recall cues you wrote in the margins are an essential step. If you use those cues to recite, you may not need study notes for some classes.

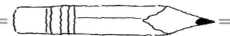

# PRACTICE

This practice will put together several of the steps.

1. Start by writing two questions for the information you read above.

   Question one: _____

   _____

   _____

   _____

   Question two: _____

   _____

   _____

   _____

2. Go back over what you read above and mark it—underline or highlight and list some recall phrases.

3. Write the answers to the two questions you made up for this reading.

   Answer to question one: _____

   _____

   _____

   _____

   _____

   Answer to question two: _____

   _____

   _____

   _____

   _____

Do your questions, markings, and answers all work together for you?

*Compare your answers with the author's suggestions in the Appendix.*

# SQ3R Step 5: Review

Once you have read an entire chapter, section by section, you are ready to review that chapter.

This is the final step in understanding the material.

1. Reread each main heading.

2. Review the underlined and highlighted material.

3. Answer the questions you formed for each section. Use your reading notes to help you review.

Practice reviewing with this book. Take a few minutes to go back through the pages of this part, reviewing the main headings and the work you did.

### Final Reading Practice

To practice putting this all together for yourself, select a chapter in one of your textbooks and mark, highlight, and make brief study notes (1 to 1 1/2 pages only).

Then ask your instructor, a tutor, or a fellow student whom you know is successful to review your notes with the underlining and recall cues in the margins, and have that person make suggestions for improvement.

# A Lifetime Habit: Careful Reading

Whatever your age, it is important to make a habit of reading. You are never too young or too old to make reading an important part of your life. Reading for pleasure is as important as critical reading for learning.

As you study and plan for further learning, compile a list of books that would be helpful in meeting your goals. Ask teachers, librarians, and fellow students for ideas. Some teachers provide lists of suggested reading beyond actual assignments—always try to include at least one or two of them in your study plan. The earlier in your academic career you begin reading, the better.

Begin reading newspapers, magazines, and online material regularly and build your vocabulary as you go along. Oprah Winfrey has said that her stern father had her learn 20 new words and write one book report a week. Her grandmother taught her to read at 2 years old. We can't all be like Oprah, but we can begin to improve our reading skills at any age—and enjoy the process!

***Tip:*** *This book includes a list of suggestions for further reading, in the Appendix. Take a moment to look at it now.*

# Your Focus Points

Do you feel that you know a lot about what you read in this part?

You probably do—because you used SQ3R to learn SQ3R. As you read and did the exercises, you probably noticed that everything in this part gave you practice in the SQ3R method.

As you can see from your work in this part, it is a process that works. Try it with all your reading assignments. It is a valuable reading tool that, with practice, will become a habit you can use all your life.

Reflect on what you learned by answering these questions, using the lines provided.

1. What ideas and suggestions were the most important for you in this part?

_____

_____

_____

_____

_____

_____

_____

2. Which suggestions do you want to focus on and practice more?

_____

_____

_____

_____

_____

_____

_____

# PART 5

# Memory Training

*"If we would have new knowledge, we must get a whole world of new questions."*

**–Susanne K. Langer, philosopher**

# Improve Your Memory

Human beings are capable of extraordinary feats of memory. In fact, experts in the study of memory agree that the skill is not all due to an inborn ability, but is developed through the use of various techniques and considerable practice.

## *Overcoming Memory Problems*

Have you studied for hours trying to memorize material for a test and then gone blank? Practicing the memory strategies in this section with help you reduce blanking out.

But if your memory-related problems seem severe, if you have difficulty focusing your attention or have severe test-taking anxiety, or if you feel you may have a learning disability, talk with your counselor or instructor. A wide variety of helpful methods and treatment options are available today. Do not hesitate—getting help if you need it will remove obstacles so you can concentrate on being a successful student.

## *Switch to "Single-Tasking"*

While you are studying and memorizing, avoid multitasking. Give your work your complete attention. Many studies have shown that multitasking does not speed up work; it only distracts you and slows you down.

Listening to music does help some people concentrate, but be sure that is true for you and that listening to music while you are learning is not just a habit you have acquired.

Turn off TV, radio, cell phones, and any other interruptions, electronic or otherwise. If you are working at a computer, have only your study material on your screen. Single-tasking will pay off for you in easier and more effective learning.

# Memory-Training Strategies

Like the experts, you too can improve your memory. In the next few pages, you will learn eight study strategies that, if you understand and practice them, can make your studying not only easier, but more rewarding. As you go along, think about which ones will work best for you, or about new ones you would like to try.

These are the eight strategies:

#1: Spread your memory work over several sessions

#2: Recite material out loud to a partner or study group

#3: Expect to remember (assume a positive attitude)

#4: Organize your material into a meaningful pattern

#5: Test and retest yourself, alone or with a study group

#6: Over-learn

#7: Use hooks, catchwords, and rhyming phrases or sentences

#8: Study before sleeping

Let's take a look at each of these strategies in more detail.

# Strategy #1: Spread Out Memory Work

Sometimes students think that the longer they study, the more they will learn. Unfortunately, the reverse is true. Shorter periods of memory work, not more than two hours each, are far superior to six hours of frantic cramming.

***Tip:*** *Reviewing memory work within 24 hours of the first study session is the most effective way to master the material.*

## *Distributed Practice*

Probably the more time you spend studying, the better, but practice is the optimum strategy. An ideal learning pattern would involve:

1. Immediate review within the short-term memory span

2. A review after the first hour

3. A short review after overnight sleeping

4. A short review after a week

5. A short review after a month

Do you know how much more you will be able to recall if you follow this schedule? Up to 88% of the material you review will be saved in your long-term memory.

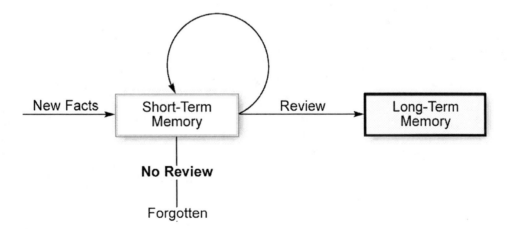

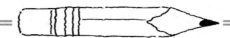

# YOUR STUDY SCHEDULE

Take a look at your study schedule, and then answer the following questions.

1. Now that you see how important it is to spread out your study, are there any changes you would make in that schedule? If so, what?

_____

_____

_____

_____

_____

_____

_____

_____

_____

2. What other changes could you make in the way you study, to help yourself do the kind of memory work suggested in this strategy?

_____

_____

_____

_____

_____

_____

_____

_____

_____

# Strategy #2: Recite Material Aloud

When you are studying or memorizing, recite the answers to your study questions aloud so that you can hear the answer. Do not simply recite the answer in your head! That is a beginning, but only a beginning. Use a study group, study partner, or a tape recorder to help.

Question yourself aloud and answer yourself aloud.

If you study in a group or with a friend, quizzing each other will improve recall. Although your memory may begin to fail on a test, the voice of the person you studied with will often come through loudly and clearly.

*Tip:* *Research studies show that answering questions aloud improves recall by at least 80%!*

## Use All Your Senses

The more senses you involve in the learning process, the longer you will remember.

**See It**      Read and visualize the material

**Say It**      Answer the questions aloud that you formulate from your class notes. Use the cues in the recall column of your textbook and your notes to help you ask yourself study questions.

**Write It**    Write answers to questions from your study notes. Outline major points from the text.

**Repeat It**   Repeat this entire process until you have mastered the material.

**Smell It**    Associate a particular smell with what you are learning—for example, smells from a science laboratory, or a pleasant scent you place nearby while studying.

# Strategy #3: Expect to Remember

*Decide* to remember! As obvious as this seems, many students fail to realize the power of intent to recall. Because you want to remember words to a favorite song, you can easily repeat the lyrics word for word.

It is amazing how much we are capable of remembering. Think about how many passwords, phone numbers, e-mail addresses, and directions to people's homes that you remember. We remember these things because we want to; it is easier to remember them than to look them up each time.

If you *want* to remember, you will. Your attitude is the secret. Believe in yourself and in your ability to learn. Remind yourself of your commitment to learning. Think of the many reasons that you are studying and why you want to remember the material you are studying—for tests, yes, but also as a part of your overall learning goals.

# Strategy #4: Organize the Material

People who recall long lists of numbers often can do so because they have found a *pattern* or a *relationship*.

## Try This

Look at this string of numbers and take a moment to try to memorize the list.

        3      6      9     12    15    18    21    24

What is the pattern in this string of numbers? Write your answer below, and then check your answer in the Appendix.

_____

_____

Learning this set of numbers was easier for you if you recognized the pattern. The same is true about anything you need to remember. Break up the material into some kind of pattern.

You did this in another way when you learned and practiced SQ3R. When you read material with the SQ3R method, your markings become a pattern that helps you organize and remember the material.

*Tip:* *Include no more than seven chunks of information in each organizational pattern. Cognitive psychologists have found that we best retain a maximum of seven chunks of information. Telephone numbers (excluding area codes) are examples of the need to limit information to seven bits for better recall.*

# Strategy #5: Test and Retest Yourself

If you had to learn 10 definitions for class tomorrow, how could you test yourself? Would you write the definitions over and over or read the list aloud 20 times? Neither method is the best choice.

Instead, follow this self-testing process:

1. Memorize the *first* item.

2. Go on to the *second* item and memorize it.

3. Now repeat the first item *and* the second by memory.

4. When you know those two, go on to the *third*.

5. Memorize the third item *and* repeat items one, two, and three.

6. Continue in this same manner until you have learned all 10 definitions.

*Tip:* **Don't forget to use all your senses: Read It! Write It! Say It! Sing It! Imagine It!**

## Try It

1. Go back to Strategy #3, Expect to Remember. Memorize something about it that is important for you and will help you study. After you have learned it, close the book for a moment and say it from memory.

2. Move on to Strategy #4, Organize the Material. Again, memorize something about this that is helpful and important to you. After you have learned it, close the book and recite *both* items you have learned, the one from Strategy #3 and the one from Strategy #4.

3. Now memorize something helpful to you from Strategy #5, Test and Retest, above. Got it? Close the book again, and recite all three items to yourself.

# Strategy #6: Over-Learn

Review material that you have learned several times. When final examinations or midterms come around, you will have mastered material that you have encoded for long-term recall. In math classes, rework the model or sample five or more times to encode the correct formula into your long-term memory.

Commercials can haunt you for years because of the repetition of a jingle or song. You have over-learned them, simply because you have heard and sung them so often—even when you did not want to. You get the same effect when you review and recite material again and again.

Over-learning can give you confidence when you are working with material that is difficult for you. As you work with it over and over, it will become familiar to you and you will be able to recall it more easily.

## Think About It

1. Can you think of a commercial, or a saying, or something else that you know you will remember because you over-learned it? Write it here.

_____

_____

_____

_____

_____

_____

2. Where would over-learning be helpful for you in the subjects you are studying?

_____

_____

_____

_____

_____

_____

# Strategy #7: Use Recall Hooks

Create hooks and catchwords that help you recall what you are memorizing. You have already seen one of them in this book: SQ3R is a hook that helps you remember the five steps of reading effectively.

You hook the idea into your memory bank by using mnemonic phrases or catchwords to pull up more information and recall the details. For example, some people use ROY G. BIV to remember the colors of the rainbow.

**Red Orange Yellow**     **Green**     **Blue Indigo Violet**

## *Making Up Catchwords*

You can create your own catchwords to go with whatever you are learning. Students working together often have fun doing this. For example, to remember the eight memory strategies in this section, you can employ a similar hooking device.

- **S**   **S**pread Out Memory Work
- **R**   **R**ecite Aloud
- **E**   **E**xpect to Remember
- **O**   **O**rganize the Material
- **T**   **T**est and Retest
- **O**   **O**ver-Learn
- **R**   **R**ecall with Hooks and Catchwords
- **S**   **S**tudy Before Sleeping

If the order is not important, you can create a catchword or phrase from the first letter of the words. The strange or bizarre is usually easier to remember.

### Try It

Create a word by scrambling the above letters from the list of memory techniques. Spend no more than five minutes thinking.

\_\_\_\_  \_\_\_\_  \_\_\_\_  \_\_\_\_  \_\_\_\_  \_\_\_\_  \_\_\_\_  \_\_\_\_

Compare your answer with the author's suggestion in the Appendix.

## *Rhyming*

If words must be remembered in a specific order, then a rhyming nonsensical sentence may help you remember. Rhymes can help you remember many types of information. When rhythm is added, the results are even better. We all know

> Thirty days hath September

> April, June, and November

Notice that the poem rhymes and has rhythm. Some students like to borrow cheers from their school's sports teams and put in new words to help memorize things like mathematical formulas.

If English is your second language, do you know rhymes or poems in your first language that you can use to help you remember what you learn? If so, go ahead and use them, as long as you know how to translate the information into English when you take a test. Using our first language can help us think in different ways about something. You might even have some fun sharing your rhymes with other students!

# Strategy #8: Study Before and After Sleep

To get the most mileage from study and memory work, try to review right before going to sleep. Cut off the television and do not become otherwise distracted.

You will process this new material while you are sleeping. As you wake, review again. To put a tight cap on the bottle of information you are encoding for future recall, review again later the same morning.

Also pay attention to what time of day is your best learning time. Although other obligations or activities may prevent you from studying at that time, try to do it whenever you can. If possible, change your study schedule sometimes to take advantage of your best study time.

# Visualize for Success

Visualizing what you study is one of the most effective ways to remember just about anything. You have heard the saying "A picture is worth a thousand words." Although you may not remember a thousand words with just one image, a picture is a powerful way to help yourself learn.

## *Use Images as Reminders*

When you read about Strategy #7, Recall Hooks, you discovered the author's suggested catchword ROOSTERS. Each letter is a signal for the first word of one of the eight memory techniques.

If you want to remember even longer, *visualize* the catchword in your mind's eye or associate the word with an object or a place with which you are already familiar. Can you remember the image of roosters in a picture book from your childhood or, even better, actual roosters that you have seen? This is a strong image that you will not forget easily.

When you can visualize items from your text or classroom notes, they are much easier to recall. The rooster visualization is an example of how to use association to remember. Simpler visual displays can be just as effective.

## Use Graphics as Reminders

Another powerful technique for recalling information is to distill it into a graphic or visual display. This technique forces you to analyze the information and arrange it in a non-textual manner. Understanding the interrelationship and connections of data makes it easier to remember. Study the following pages for examples of graphical displays you can use to organize information and improve your recall.

***Tip:*** *Association is an important technique for efficient recall.*

## Sample Graphics

You can use graphics like these as you take notes in class, when you organize your material for study, and when you want to memorize specific material. If you use your computer for studying, you can use any features you are comfortable with to create visual aids on your computer. (Just do not get so absorbed in creating graphics that you lose valuable study time.)

### Chronological Timelines

These are useful for history classes or any subject that includes time periods. College bookstores and other bookstores often have prepared timelines for study aids.

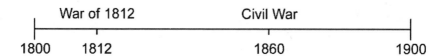

## Tree Diagrams

These are popular among biology students and genealogists, but the image can be used for many academic subjects.

Try listing five skills you've learned from this section. Fill in this tree map using the five memory strategies (from the previous pages) that are most important to you.

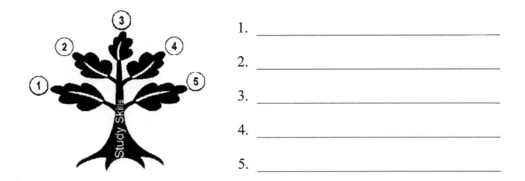

1. _____

2. _____

3. _____

4. _____

5. _____

## Flow Chart

Flow charts are helpful for math, project management, or any subject matter that includes a sequence of steps.

## Study Map

Use a study map to show how various points relate to a main topic. This is especially helpful for subjects like management, social studies, or others that include discussion of ideas or that require you to organize your thinking around a specific concept.

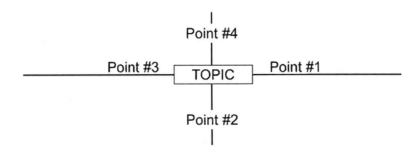

## Sun Shapes or Clocks

Patterns like these help you remember sequences, particularly sequences that run in cycles. Examples are economic cycles, business cycles, and life cycles.

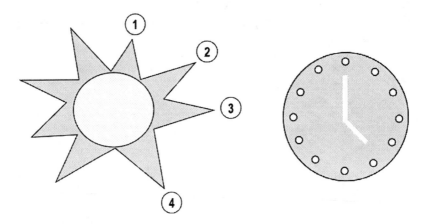

## Clustering or Branching Lines

These are useful for grouping ideas when you need to remember them to present in an organized way, such as an essay exam or a class presentation.

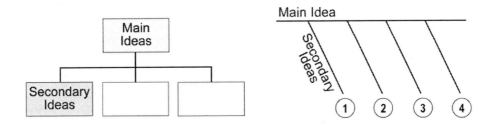

## Hand Prints

Hand prints are a simple visual you can use for any topic when you need to remember ideas or concepts of equal importance. You can also use this device when you are giving a speech. Visualize a key word on each finger.

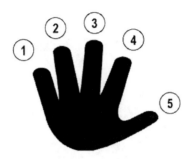

## Loci Method

The ancient Greeks used the rooms of a house (*loci* is Latin for "location") to help remember the points of a speech. You can do the same by walking through the front door and visualizing your introduction, move into the living room for your first point, and so on.

The point is that we can link new information more easily on to a previous memory, like our homes or even parts of our cars. Use whatever is the most vivid and familiar "memory structure" for you as you apply the loci method.

# PRACTICE USING MEMORY PATTERNS

**Exercise 1:**

On the left, list the subjects you are now studying. On the right, write one or two of the memory patterns that would help you remember what you learn in that subject.

| Subject | Patterns that would help you remember |
| --- | --- |
| _____ | _____ |
| _____ | _____ |
| _____ | _____ |
| _____ | _____ |
| _____ | _____ |
| _____ | _____ |
| _____ | _____ |

**Exercise 2:**

Map a chapter from a text, a lecture, or other material that you are currently studying. Use one or more of the pattern techniques.

*Tip:* *Color helps! It creates a stronger "glue" for your mind and is highly recommended by cognitive psychologists. It is also sometimes more fun!*

# Review of Memory Techniques

## The Eight Memory Strategies

1. Spread memory work over several sessions

2. Recite material out loud

3. Expect to remember (assume a positive attitude)

4. Organize the material into a meaningful pattern

5. Test and retest yourself

6. Over-learn

7. Recall: use hooks, catchwords, and rhyming

8. Study before sleeping and upon awakening

## Visualize for Success

➤ Use chronological timelines to remember dates

➤ Sketch trees and fill in the branches with material to be learned

➤ Use flow charts to remember a sequence

➤ Create a study map

➤ Make sun shapes or clocks to remember the relation of various items

➤ Cluster thoughts in an outline format

➤ When there are 10 or fewer items to learn, use hand prints

➤ Use the loci method

*Tip:* **Review this section of study skills strategies often.**

**Building Your Skills**

On the lines below, list the three ideas about memory that you want to work on to build your learning skills.

_____

_____

_____

_____

# P A R T 6

# Exam Strategies

*To be able to be caught up into the world of thought—that is to be educated."*

**–Edith Hamilton, educator, writer, and historian**

# Taking Tests Well

Kayla was a typical student who faced a common challenge—three major tests and a final examination would account for 60% of her final grade. Often Kayla blanked out on exams and found it difficult to finish during the time allotted. If you have felt this test-taking anxiety, you are not alone.

Successful students learn sound strategies for taking tests. After you have a good understanding of taking classroom notes, reading your textbook, and memory training, you are ready to "score" by learning test-taking strategies.

Relaxation tapes and techniques can also reduce stress and can be an enormous help to you. Relaxation is crucial for optimum learning, so try a few deep breaths before you begin to study or as you start a test. Some researchers have found that playing Baroque music is particularly helpful for learning at home or in the classroom. If Baroque music does not appeal to you, try something soothing and calming. This creates a linkage between the right and left brain and establishes an emotive link with the material.

| **LEFT BRAIN** emphasizes: | | **RIGHT BRAIN** emphasizes: |
|---|---|---|
| language | | forms and patterns |
| mathematical formulae | | special manipulation |
| logic | | rhythm and musical appreciation |
| numbers | | images/pictures |
| sequence | | imagination |
| linearity | | daydreaming |
| analysis | | dimension |
| words of a song | | tune of a song |

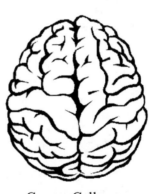

Corpus Callosum

# Mastering Objective Tests

To do well on an objective test, you need to memorize facts and thoroughly understand concepts and relationships. The following hints should help you score higher on true-false and matching type questions. Use your instructor as a resource. Ask what type of questions will be on the test, and then prepare accordingly.

**NOTE:** Use the same tips when you are taking tests online. If your instructor permits, have pencil and paper with you to write down key words or work out possible answers.

## Some Hints:

➢ **Look over the entire test.** Know how much each question is worth and budget your time accordingly. Check the clock every 10 minutes to ensure you will not be caught off guard and run out of time. If necessary, put your watch on the desk in front of you.

➢ **Answer the easiest questions first.** Put a check by those that are harder and return to those questions last. Otherwise, you will waste valuable time and miss answering the easier questions. Place another line through the check when you complete the harder questions.

➢ **Underline key words in the question.** Make special note of negative words like *not*. Feel free, however, to ask for clarification from your instructor if the question is vague or unclear.

## *Matching Questions*

Approach matching-question testing as a game and play by the rules.

Rule # 1    As always, begin by reading the question and underlining or numbering key words.

Rule # 2    Glance over both columns quickly. Which column has the longer entries? Begin looking at that side so you can save time as you scan the shorter column for an answer each time.

Rule # 3    Warning! Do not select an answer unless you are certain you have selected a correct match. Why? Because you have substantially reduced the number of items left for the more difficult final matches.

Rule # 4    Circle or draw a line through each answer that you eliminate.

Rule # 5    As you eliminate the matches you are sure of, use your best guess for the correct answer. It is okay to guess at this point.

## *True-False Questions*

➤ Answers containing such words as *all*, *never*, *always*, and *everyone* usually are wrong.

➤ On the other hand, qualifiers such as *frequently*, *probably*, and *generally* more often indicate a true answer.

**Example**

T  F  Class notes should *always* be rewritten.

The word *always* is a clue that the answer may be false.

## *Multiple-Choice Questions*

1. Draw a line through each answer that you eliminate. (See example below.)

2. Ensure that the grammatical structure of the question agrees with your choice.

3. Read all choices. Even if the first answer seems correct, another choice may be better, or "all of the above" may be the correct response.

4. If you are at a complete loss, and there is no penalty for guessing, choose the longest answer—especially on teacher-made exams.

5. When opposite statements appear in a question, one of the statements is often correct.

**Example**

When two opposite statements appear in a multiple-choice question—

  a. one of the opposite statements is usually correct.

  b. ~~neither are correct.~~

  c. ~~both are correct.~~

  d. ~~choice in the middle is often correct.~~

# Excelling on Essay Exams

Do essay exams create more anxiety for you than objective exams? Fear of unknown essay questions can be substantially reduced if you follow these four simple steps:

**Step 1:** Develop your own practice essay questions by looking over your lecture notes and textbook assignments and guessing what the instructor would select. Write a practice essay and read it out loud. Also recite out loud other compositions that you can write at home.

**Step 2:** Sketch out a variety of outline responses to 10 or more possible questions.

**Step 3:** Memorize the outlines using catchphrases or mnemonic (memory) devices.

**Step 4:** Practice writing an essay within a specific time constraint. This is especially helpful if you have difficulty completing your tests within the prescribed time.

## *Improving Specific Essay Skills*

Besides using the above steps to review and prepare for essay tests, you can use the following skills to help you succeed on essay exams:

➤ Essay Skill #1: Budget Your Time

➤ Essay Skill #2: Analyze Key Words

➤ Essay Skill #3: Create an Outline

➤ Essay Skill #4: Focus Your Essay

➤ Essay Skill #5: Build Strong Paragraphs

➤ Essay Skill #6: Use Transition Words

Use these skills and suggestions whether you write your essay by hand or on a computer. When you use a computer, have pencil and paper with you if your instructor permits. Use it to sketch out and organize your ideas.

**NOTE:** You can use these essay exam skills for writing any essay assignment, even when it is not a test. Building these skills will help you think in a more organized way, strengthen your writing, and improve your study skills overall.

# Essay Skill #1: Budget Your Time

Take a few minutes to look over the entire test and budget your time accordingly. Are the required answers all of equal length, or will you have to write longer or shorter answers for some questions? Note in the margins about how many minutes you want to use for each answer.

Check to see if your instructor has noted how many points an answer is worth. For example, if one question is worth 30 points, you want to give yourself plenty of time to work with it. If a question is worth 5 points, you can leave it till later in the test.

As you skim through the test, if key words or ideas come to you, you can jot them in the margins. Do not stop to fully answer the question at this time.

Decide which questions to answer first. It is usually best to start with those you know well, because you can accumulate points that way. Be sure, however, that answering all the easier ones first will not take time away from questions that are worth more points.

# Essay Skill #2: Analyze Key Words

As you work on each question, read it carefully and underline key words. Think about what the question is asking you to do. For example, if you are asked to "trace" the development of social reform in America, you need to describe the historical development of the subject. On the other hand, if you are asked to "criticize" or "critique" a poem or book, your instructor expects you to show the positive and negative points and support your ideas with evidence.

If you are using a computer to take your test, and you have blank paper available, you can jot down the key words for each question as you go along. Or, if the system you are using permits, you can highlight or underline on the screen. (Some test-taking systems do not permit the user to change or mark the questions in any way.)

## *Key Words to Learn*

Here are some other key words that often appear in essay exams or assignments.

| | | |
|---|---|---|
| evaluate | prove | illustrate |
| analyze | relate | diagram |
| delineate | state | discuss |
| compare | justify | enumerate |
| describe | evaluate | illustrate |

If you are not familiar with these words, look them up in a dictionary. Then try the matching exercise on the next page.

# ESSAY EXAM MATCHING QUIZ

The following words are frequently used in essay examinations. Match the word to the appropriate definition.

**Hint:** Remember the suggestions for taking matching quizzes and use them for this quiz.

| | | | |
|---|---|---|---|
| _____ | 1. summarize | A. | Show good reasons for |
| _____ | 2. evaluate | B. | Establish the truth of something by giving factual evidence or logical reasons |
| _____ | 3. contrast | C. | Use a word picture, a diagram, a chart, or a concrete example to clarify a point |
| _____ | 4. explain | D. | Talk over; consider from various points of view |
| _____ | 5. describe | E. | Make plain; give your meaning of; translate |
| _____ | 6. define | F. | Sum up; give the main points briefly |
| _____ | 7. compare | G. | Give an account of; tell about; give a word picture of |
| _____ | 8. discuss | H. | Make clear; interpret; make plain; tell "how" to do |
| _____ | 9. criticize | I. | Give the meaning of a word or concept; place it in the class to which it belongs and set it off from other items |
| _____ | 10. justify | J. | Bring out points of similarity and points of difference |
| _____ | 11. trace | K. | Bring out the points of difference |
| _____ | 12. interpret | L. | Follow the course of; follow the trail of |
| _____ | 13. prove | M. | State your opinion of the correctness or merit of an item or issue |
| _____ | 14. illustrate | N. | Give the good points and the bad ones; appraise |

*Compare your answers with the author's in the Appendix.*

# Essay Skill #3: Create an Outline

Before you start writing, create an informal outline of the main ideas and supporting detail that you need to answer the question. You may feel that you do not have time for this, but taking a moment or two to create an outline will make it easier for you to answer the question. It will also help ensure that you cover all the important points.

Are you using a computer to write your test? Then create your outline on blank paper if your instructor allows it, or do it in the answer space onscreen if you can. You can delete it after you finish answering if space is a problem.

Some students use a "cluster" outline similar to the one illustrated. You can also use any other pattern that works for you. This cluster outline shows the three essay skills you have reviewed so far.

**CLUSTER OUTLINE**

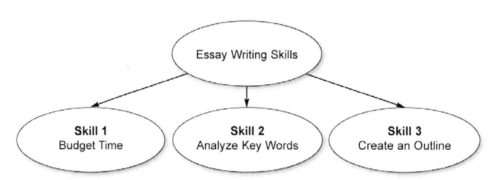

# Essay Skill #4: Focus Your Essay

Strive for a focused essay. The most common complaint from teachers is that essays they read are too general and do not provide adequate support for the ideas presented.

Avoid common focusing problems by following these tips:

| Common Error | How to Correct It |
|---|---|
| 1. Padding | State your main point and stick to it. Avoid all extraneous material. Follow your thesis or central point. |
| 2. Weak development | Develop three main points. Provide details, examples, and/or statistics. Do not simply generalize without supporting details. |
| 3. Choppiness | Use transition words to ensure that your essay is more coherent. Transition words will show relationships between sentences and paragraphs. Remember that too many simple sentences will give the paragraph a choppy "sound." |
| 4. Comma faults, fragments, run-on sentences | Put a period in place of the comma. Pay special attention to writing complete sentence and avoiding fragments. Practice sentence structure and get grammar help if needed. |

Now use the exercise on the next page to review Skills 3 and 4.

# CLUSTERING

Practice clustering, Skill #3, using the information for Skill #4, focusing.

Look at the following essay question. Remember to pay attention to the key words! Then create a cluster diagram that you might use to outline your answer for this question on a test.

**ESSAY QUESTION:** Describe three of the four common errors found in students' writing and explain how to correct these mistakes.

Draw your diagram in the space below.

*When you have finished, compare your diagram with the author's suggestion in the Appendix.*

# Essay Skill #5: Build Strong Paragraphs

Make sure your paragraphs have a topic sentence, which states the main idea, and a thesis, which is the central idea you are writing about. Be sure that your topic sentence relates to your thesis in an organized way. Look at this example:

*Cell phones have a variety of uses: making calls, sending text messages and e-mails, taking photos, and other uses depending on the phone you buy.*

After you read that sentence, you expect that the writer will give more details about the various uses of cell phones. This writer's topic is the uses of cell phones, and this topic sentence states it clearly.

The sample sentence above could be the first sentence of an answer to questions like the following:

➤ *Describe the various uses of cell phones.*

➤ *Compare the various uses of cell phones according to which are most useful for parents.*

➤ *Explain why cell phones have become so popular.*

## Organizing Paragraphs

Every sentence in your paragraph should relate to the topic and thesis in some way. Remember Skill #2: analyze the key words in the question. Then build your paragraphs to do what the key words indicate.

There are a variety of organizational patterns you can use for your paragraphs or essay, depending on the question. Some examples are classification, cause and effect, pros and cons, advantages and disadvantages, anecdote (short story), cataloguing, and chronological sequence.

Continue to add paragraphs as needed to completely answer the question. Your instructor may give you a limit or range for the number of paragraphs; if so, stick to that limit.

## Writing a Conclusion

End with a clear conclusion. This can be a single sentence if you are writing a brief essay, or it can be a short paragraph of its own if you are writing a longer essay. Your conclusion should restate the thesis and summarize your ideas. For example:

*Looking at all the uses and features of cell phones I have described, it's easy to see why cell phones are so popular. They provide something for just about anyone's communication needs, are convenient to carry, and can be fun to use.*

# Essay Skill #6: Use Transition Words

Transition words have two purposes. They connect sentences or paragraphs. They also signal a relationship between what comes before and what goes after the transition word.

Transitions make your writing flow smoothly. Be sure to use them, but do not overdo it. Use no more than three in each paragraph, as a general rule.

Look at these examples:

*Sentence structure problems can take away from the focus of an essay. Therefore, it is important to brush up on your grammar if needed to build your essay skills.*

*In conclusion, if you pay attention to the specific essay skills in this section, you can write stronger and more focused essays.*

In the first example, *therefore* indicates that the first sentence is the reason for what is stated in the second sentence.

In the second example, *in conclusion* signifies that you are now writing your final paragraph or sentence.

## *Examples of Transition Words*

| | | |
|---|---|---|
| therefore | furthermore | consequently |
| moreover | of course | on the other hand |
| first | in conclusion | nevertheless |
| since | in addition | admittedly |
| also | finally | thus |
| first of all | next | assuredly |

Remember that these transition words can be used at the beginning of a sentence or in the middle, depending on what to emphasize; but less effectively at the end. When the transition words come at the end of the sentence, they often fail to serve their purpose and may sound unnecessary.

For example:

➤ The human heart weighs less than a pound. On the other hand, the brain weighs three pounds [emphasis on contrast between the two organs].

➤ The human brain weighs less than a pound. The brain, on the other hand, weighs only three pounds [emphasis on the brain].

➤ The human brain weighs less than a pound. The brain weighs only three pounds, on the other hand [purpose of "on the other hand" is lost].

# PRACTICE WITH TRANSITION WORDS

In this exercise you will review Skills #5 and #6: Build strong paragraphs, and use transition words.

Write a paragraph of about five sentences using the information from the picture and text below. Incorporate at least two of the transition words from the list on the preceding page.

**Your Brain…**

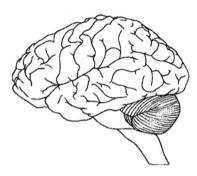

**A three-pound universe!**

You have at least 100 billion nerve cells (neurons) in your brain.

Each of these neurons makes between 5,000 and 50,000 contacts with other neurons.

Write your paragraph in this space.

_____

_____

_____

_____

_____

_____

_____

*Compare your writing with the author's suggestions in the Appendix.*

# Additional Preparation Strategies

By now you have learned specific strategies for mastering objective tests and excelling on essay exams. This part explains additional strategies you can employ to improve your preparation for taking tests in general. Let's look at these now.

## *Study Sheets*

A study sheet has the questions on one page and the answers on another, as shown in the sample below. Or you can use one page and divide it down the middle with the questions to the left and the answers to the right.

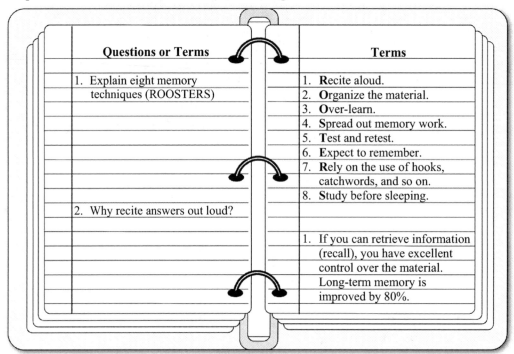

| Questions or Terms | Terms |
|---|---|
| 1. Explain eight memory techniques (ROOSTERS) | 1. **Recite** aloud.<br>2. **Organize** the material.<br>3. **Over**-learn.<br>4. **Spread** out memory work.<br>5. **Test** and retest.<br>6. **Expect** to remember.<br>7. **Rely** on the use of hooks, catchwords, and so on.<br>8. **Study** before sleeping. |
| 2. Why recite answers out loud? | 1. If you can retrieve information (recall), you have excellent control over the material. Long-term memory is improved by 80%. |

### Using Study Sheets

➤ After writing or reciting answers to the questions several times, you are ready to cover the answers and use a blank page to write the answers from memory.

➤ If you can answer the question correctly, without looking at the answer, place a check (√) by the question.

➤ If you cannot recall the answer, look at it and try again.

➤ Repeat this process until you have mastered the material.

# Study Cards

Some students use 3-by-5-inch index cards to help them study. Cards may be used for mathematics, science, English, history, or almost any academic subject. Study cards are easy to carry with you anywhere, giving you the opportunity to study whenever you have a few moments.

Some students punch a hole in the top left-hand corner of the cards and hold them all together with a metal ring. And some bookstores and office-supply stores sell "systems" for organizing cards, which include smaller cards of various colors and a notebook designed to hold the cards.

***Tip:*** *Flash cards are especially effective for studying a foreign language or ESL.*

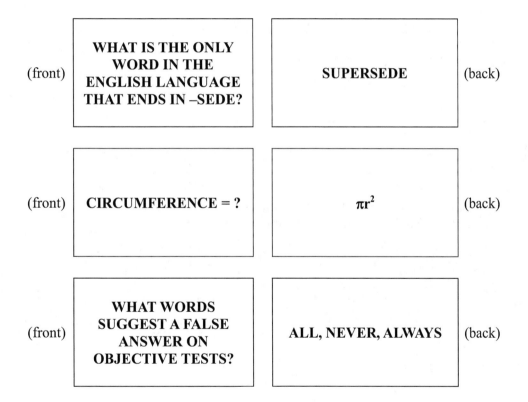

(front) **WHAT IS THE ONLY WORD IN THE ENGLISH LANGUAGE THAT ENDS IN –SEDE?**   **SUPERSEDE** (back)

(front) **CIRCUMFERENCE = ?**   $\pi r^2$ (back)

(front) **WHAT WORDS SUGGEST A FALSE ANSWER ON OBJECTIVE TESTS?**   **ALL, NEVER, ALWAYS** (back)

### Using Study Cards

**Step 1:** Look at the front side of the card and ask yourself the question.

**Step 2:** Answer the question or define the concept. Then turn the card over to see if you are correct.

**Step 3:** Correct? Place the card in a stack to your left, or mark it somehow in pencil (so you can erase the mark later).

**Step 4:** Incorrect? Test and retest three times. Put that card in a stack to your right, or mark it.

**Step 5:** Have someone else ask you the questions repeating Steps 1–5.

## Save Quizzes and Tests

Save every quiz or test you take. Go over the questions you missed until you are sure of the answers. Ask for help from your instructor, a tutor, or a study partner to help you improve before the next test. You can also use all quizzes, tests, and other papers you have written to help you review for midterms or final exams.

## Remember Other Parts of Your Grade

Generally, a test score is not the only item included in your overall grade for a class. So if you have difficulty with one test, do not give up. Use each test as a chance to review and strengthen your skills in that particular subject. At the beginning of each course, if the teacher does not provide information on what is required and what is counted toward the final grade, ask about it.

# Exam Strategies Review

Use this list to review the exam strategies you have learned. Check [√] those you plan to practice.

## For objective tests:

❑ Answer easiest questions first.

❑ Underline key words in each question.

❑ Cross out answers you have eliminated.

❑ Be alert for words such as *always* and *never*.

❑ Ensure that the grammatical structure of the answer is consistent with the question.

❑ If there is no penalty for guessing, answer every question.

## For essay exams:

❑ Anticipate questions the instructor might ask.

❑ Sketch a variety of outline responses to model questions.

❑ Practice writing sample essays.

❑ Analyze the entire test and budget your time before beginning to write.

❑ Read each question carefully and underline key words.

❑ Create an informal cluster outline of your response before starting to write. If you choose, you can simply number your main points.

❑ Strive for a focused essay, tightly organized and supported with facts.

❑ Make sure your paragraphs have main idea sentences (topic sentence) and a thesis (central idea). Be sure your topic sentences relate to the thesis in an organized way.

❑ Use a paragraph structure that goes with the essay test question. Use the key words in the question as your guide.

❑ Add a conclusion to your essay or paragraph. The conclusion should relate to the essay test question.

# PART 7

# Studying Mathematics and Related Subjects

# Math Tips, Techniques, and Ideas

Mathematics requires special study techniques. This brief part will provide a few tips and ideas for improving your math study skills.

The ideas in this part apply to any subject in which mathematical thinking is part of the work. For example, accounting, economics, some business classes, project management, physics, engineering, and similar subjects all require mathematical thinking and learning as you study them.

## *Give Math Special Attention*

With its abstract structures, patterns, and relationships, the study of mathematics and math-related subjects requires different techniques from those used in other subjects. Apply these guidelines to help you through the complexities:

➤ Copy all the instructor's theorems, principles, and definitions *exactly*. Do not paraphrase or condense anything that is written on the board. Also be sure to copy the instructor's explanation. Draw arrows to the explanation for each step of the problem.

➤ Because it may be difficult to take notes on the instructor's explanation and copy the problem off the board at the same time, you may want to record the instructor's explanation (always ask the instructor's permission for this). Also ask if there are related study aids that your teacher recommends.

➤ Plan to spend extra time on your math homework if math is a difficult subject for you, if it is your major, or if it is a critical part of a math-related subject you are taking. Pay attention to what this might do to your study schedule and adjust as needed. Some teachers set aside part of each class to let students start homework, so students can get help with understanding concepts or difficult points. If your teacher does this, take full advantage of it.

➤ If math is difficult for you, you may find it necessary to ask for special help. If you become confused or lost, seek the assistance of your instructor or a tutor. Mathematics often builds on a set of rules; and if you do not understand basic principles, the likelihood is that once you get lost, you will stay lost. Ask for help as soon as you need it instead of waiting until things get worse.

# The Five Rs of Math

Master these five techniques and you will be well on your way to math success. You may feel that doing all these steps for every math assignment will take too much time. Indeed, it may take more time at first than you are accustomed to spending on math assignments. But stay with it—you will soon see results in the way you learn, and you will find it easier to study for exams.

The following pages will give you details on these five techniques and help you rate your use of them.

> ➤ **R1:** Recopy your notes. Rewrite math notes each day in ink for clarity and permanence. Neatness is especially important because of the need for accuracy.

> ➤ **R2:** Rework the model. This is the crucial step that most students overlook. Instead of figuring out what is being taught in the model problem, they jump right into doing homework and end up reworking problems several times. Instead, rework model problems over and over until you can do them without stopping.

> ➤ **R3:** Recite out loud. Work with a study partner and force each other to explain out loud each step of the process.

> ➤ **R4:** Recheck your work. Recheck your thinking process as well by listening to your "mind chatter."

> ➤ **R5:** Test answers for Reasonableness. Does your answer to the problem make sense?

# THE FIVE RS OF MATH

To help you understand the Five Rs of Math, read the descriptions in this exercise and write notes in the margin or recall cues to the left of each one. These notes should help you remember what is most important to you in each tip.

**RECALL
CUES**

——————

——————

——————

$R_1$ **Recopy** your notes in pen. Color-code definitions, rules, and problem areas discussed by your instructor. Neatness and legibility are your first steps toward becoming a better math student.

> How do you rate your math notes?
>
> ❑ Organized and clear
>
> ❑ Messy
>
> ❑ Disorganized but neat

——————

——————

——————

$R_2$ **Rework** the model or example over and over until you can do it without hesitation.

> Have you ever taken this step before beginning your homework?
>
> ❑ YES    ❑ NO
>
> If not, try it for a week and see if it makes a difference.

CONTINUED

**RECALL
CUES**

**R**₃ **Recite.** Oral recitation will improve your mathematical skills. Practice this step with a study partner or friend. Force each other to explain out loud each step of the process. If you are studying alone, still express your thinking aloud.

Have you ever taken this step while doing your homework?

❑ YES ❑ NO

If not, try it for a week and see if it makes a difference.

**R**₄ **Recheck** your computations. Also recheck your thinking process. This is even more important when you move from one step of a problem to the next or from one concept to a new one.

"Mind Chatter"[1]

Questioning and recording the internal thinking of professionals revealed the following internal dialogues were common:

1. "Let me read the question again to be sure what's being asked. I'll circle or underline the question."

2. "Okay. I see, but I'll read it again to be sure."

3. "Slow down. Don't rush."

4. "What is given? What is known?"

5. "How can I diagram, make a chart, or draw a visual to help me?"

Lawyers, doctors, engineers, and similar professionals were always painstakingly careful to reread phrases and double-check their work.

[1] Adapted from *Problem Solving and Comprehension* by Arthur Whimbey and Jack Lochhead.

═══ CONTINUED ═══

**RECALL CUES**

_____

_____

R₅

_____

Test for **Reasonableness.** Plug your answer in to the problem to see if it makes sense. This final check could save you time and embarrassment later.

> Asking questions about how reasonable an answer is will make critical thinking a habit and problem solving less ominous.

*Compare your recall cues with the author's suggestions in the Appendix.*

# Tips for Computer Learning

Computer-assisted learning works well for math and related subjects, because of the specific concepts and calculations required for these subjects. Here are some suggestions for getting the most out of learning math with a computer:

➤ If your text comes with a supplementary disk, use it. It will give you extra practice and added help in learning difficult concepts.

➤ If your school has a math lab, visit it to see what is available. Teachers or tutors may be on hand to assist you.

➤ Ask your instructor if there are any computer-assisted learning programs that would help you. Check your campus or local bookstore for added resources.

➤ If you are taking an online math course, work the problems on paper as well. This will give you added practice and will help you remember what you are learning. It will also provide study notes for preparing for exams.

➤ If you need to take a math test online, have pencils and blank paper with you if your instructor allows. Use them to work out problems before entering your answer on the computer. On paper, you can check your answers before you submit them—something you cannot always do online depending on the testing program.

➤ Do not count on the speed of the computer to get you through a test or assignment any faster—you still need to do all the thinking at the pace of your own brain.

# Math Strategies Review

## *Math Study Skill Tips*

➤ Copy all theorems, principles, and definitions carefully and exactly.

➤ Record the instructor's explanation and ask about related study aids.

➤ Plan extra time if needed for math homework.

➤ Ask for help as soon as you begin having problems.

## *The Five Rs of Math*

➤ $R_1$ – **Recopy** your notes.

➤ $R_2$ – **Rework** model problems.

➤ $R_3$ – **Recite** aloud to explain each step of the problem-solving process.

➤ $R_4$ – **Recheck** your work.

➤ $R_5$ – Test your answers for **Reasonableness**—ensure your answer makes sense.

## *What Do You Need to Practice?*

On the lines below, write the three most important points for you to practice from the list above, for your math or math-related subjects.

1. _____

2. _____

3. _____

# Putting It
# All Together

# On Your Own

CONGRATULATIONS! You have done a lot of work on study skills to get to this point. To help you continue on your own, this section will take you through a review quiz, an action plan, and a checklist on study skills.

How can you continue to make progress? How can you learn to be a skillful student as well as a critical thinker? How can you use this information to improve your grades? Those are all questions you want to think about as you do the review and checklist and plan your next steps for effective learning.

Notice that the review quiz that starts on the next page has two parts: objective questions and an essay question. As you do the quiz, remember what you learned about how to work with those two types of test questions.

# FINAL REVIEW QUIZ: MULTIPLE CHOICE

Choose the best possible multiple-choice, fill-in-the-blank, or true-false answer.

1. Notes should be reviewed within:
   a. 72 hours
   b. 24 hours
   c. 48 hours
   d. None of the above

2. When two opposite statements appear in a multiple-choice question:
   a. One of the opposite statements is usually correct
   b. Neither is correct
   c. Both are correct
   d. The choice in the middle is often correct

3. Recall cues are placed in the _____ margin of the paper.

4. Reciting answers to study questions improves memory by:
   a. 82%
   b. 95%
   c. 70%
   d. None of the above

5. Study time should be divided into blocks of three to four hours.　　　T　F

6. All notes should be rewritten or typed except for math notes.　　　T　F

7. Visual patterns such as trees and clocks are useful for　　　T　F
   memorizing mathematical subjects only.

8. "Mind chatter" is "internal dialogue" used by professional　　　T　F
   problem solvers to find solutions.

9. Read through a paragraph before you underline or highlight.　　　T　F

10. SQ3R is a reading strategy developed for surveying and　　　T　F
    skimming easy material.

Now go on to the essay part of the quiz. You may check your answers for both this and the essay after you have completed both.

# FINAL REVIEW QUIZ: ESSAY PORTION

To do this portion of the quiz, look back through the book to find the ideas and suggestions that were most important to you for improving your study skills. Then answer the following essay question. As you write, you will be developing an action plan for yourself.

## Question:

List and describe the three or four suggestions in this book that are the most important ones for you to practice.

Explain why each one is important for you, and what difference it will make in your studying.

Describe how and when you will take action on this.

Use this page and the next page to write your answer.

_____

_____

_____

_____

_____

_____

_____

_____

_____

_____

_____

_____

_____

_____

_____

CONTINUED

Continue writing your essay on this page.

_____

_____

_____

_____

_____

_____

_____

_____

_____

_____

_____

_____

_____

_____

_____

_____

_____

_____

_____

_____

_____

When you have completed your essay, check the Appendix for the author's answers to the matching quiz and the author's comments on this essay. You may want to show this essay to a teacher, adviser, or someone else who is helping you learn. Post a copy of your essay where you can see it, to remind you of your commitment.

# Your Study Skills Checklist

This checklist is designed to help you review your study habits and get help with any areas where you need assistance. Once these problem areas have been identified, you can review sections of this book, or use other resources suggested by those helping you.

You will notice that this checklist has one set of directions for you, and another set of directions for your teacher, adviser, tutor, or other helper. Follow the directions to do your work first. Then select the person who will assist you, and ask that person to follow the directions to review your work. When both of you have finished, get together and discuss the results and any further actions that would be helpful to you.

You will probably get more out of this checklist if you have someone else review it with you. In some circumstances, however, this may not be possible or might not be the most practical approach. You can simply do it on your own and decide where you want to take action.

## *To the Student:*

Go through the checklist, marking YES or NO for each question. If you need or want to take action on any item, make a check in the ACTION NEEDED column. You may want to take action on a particular item even if you answered YES for it; you may want to practice that skill more. On the other hand, you do not need to take action on every item you mark NO; choose the items that you think are most important for you to work on.

## *To the Teacher, Tutor, or Adviser:*

When you receive the completed checklist from your student, first review it on your own. If you differ with the student on any of the responses, note your response in a different color. If you want to emphasize any point the student has marked for action, or you want to suggest action on something the student has not marked, then mark the ACTION NEEDED column, also with a different color.

**NOTE:** The "I" in the questions is the student.

# CHECKLIST FOR STUDY SKILLS

Student: _____   Date: _____

Adviser: _____   Date: _____

|   YES   |   NO   | **Time Management** | ACTION<br>NEEDED |
|---------|--------|---------------------|------------------|
| _____ | _____ | 1. Did I have a weekly time schedule for classes, study, and other activities? | _____ |
| _____ | _____ | 2. Do I have a copy of all my course requirements, including syllabus, deadlines for papers, midterms, and finals? | _____ |
| _____ | _____ | 3. Do I have short-term goals for my learning? | _____ |
| _____ | _____ | 4. Have I set aside a quiet place to study and do class work, where I have all the equipment and materials I need? | _____ |

### Note Taking

|   |   |   |   |
|---|---|---|---|
| _____ | _____ | 1. Do I regularly review my notes and identify strengths and weaknesses? | _____ |
| _____ | _____ | 2. Have I reviewed the model for recall cues and do I use these cues for studying? | _____ |
| _____ | _____ | 3. Am I able to answer questions or find solutions to problems using my notes to prompt me? | _____ |
| _____ | _____ | 4. Have I related lecture notes to textbook or other reading assignments? | _____ |
| _____ | _____ | 5. Do I know and use different techniques to study my notes? | _____ |

|  YES | NO | **Critical Reading Skills** | ACTION NEEDED |
|------|-----|-----|-----|
| ——— | ——— | 1. Do I mark my textbooks as I read? | ——— |
| ——— | ——— | 2. Do I read assignments before class? | ——— |
| ——— | ——— | 3. Do I know the value of the SQ3R method; and if so, am I using it? If not, why not? | ——— |

## SQ3R

**Survey**

| YES | NO | | ACTION NEEDED |
|-----|-----|-----|-----|
| ——— | ——— | 1. Do I know how to survey the entire chapter before reading the assignment? | ——— |

**Question**

| YES | NO | | ACTION NEEDED |
|-----|-----|-----|-----|
| ——— | ——— | 2. Do I ask or write questions about the text as I survey? | ——— |
| ——— | ——— | 3. Do I then read for answers to those questions? | ——— |
| ——— | ——— | 4. Do I list questions I do not understand after reading the text? | ——— |
| ——— | ——— | 5. Do I attempt to answer all questions before going to the next topic, section, or chapter? | ——— |

| YES | NO | Read and Underline | ACTION NEEDED |
|-----|-----|-----|-----|
| ――― | ――― | 6. Do I focus on the readings thoroughly and carefully, and highlight key concepts? | ――― |
| ――― | ――― | 7. Can I find the topic sentences in a paragraph? | ――― |
| ――― | ――― | 8. Do I use highlighters for a specific purpose (e.g., vocabulary, main ideas)? | ――― |
| ――― | ――― | 9. Do I use special markings or symbols to identify important points or organization? | ――― |
| ――― | ――― | 10. Do I know how to summarize a chapter by outlining or visually organizing the material with flow charts and the like? | ――― |

**Recite and Write**

| YES | NO | | ACTION NEEDED |
|-----|-----|-----|-----|
| ――― | ――― | 11. Do I understand and use recitation to help with recall and long-term memory? | ――― |
| ――― | ――― | 12. Do I write out questions I do not understand or cannot answer? | ――― |

**Review**

| YES | NO | | ACTION NEEDED |
|-----|-----|-----|-----|
| ――― | ――― | 13. Do I review my reading? If so, how? | ――― |
| ――― | ――― | 14. Do I write study notes from my reading? | ――― |

| YES | NO | **Memory Training** | ACTION NEEDED |
|---|---|---|---|
| ———— | ———— | 1. Do I spread out my memory work instead of doing it all at once? | ———— |
| ———— | ———— | 2. Do I recite, over-learn, and test myself as I memorize? | ———— |
| ———— | ———— | 3. Do I use hooks, catchphrases, and rhymes to help me memorize? | ———— |
| ———— | ———— | 4. Do I create visuals to help me remember specific material? | ———— |

| | | **Exam Strategies** | |
|---|---|---|---|
| ———— | ———— | 1. Do I review each test question before attempting to answer it? | ———— |
| ———— | ———— | 2. Am I overly anxious about test taking? If so, have I found ways to help myself relax? | ———— |
| ———— | ———— | 3. Do I budget time wisely while taking an exam? | ———— |
| ———— | ———— | 4. Do I answer easy questions first and go back through the exam to answer the more difficult questions last? | ———— |
| ———— | ———— | 5. Do I understand how to identify key words in exam directions, and do I know how to prepare a "cluster" outline for writing an essay? | ———— |

| YES | NO | **Math and Related Subjects** | ACTION NEEDED |
|-----|-----|-----|-----|
| ——— | ——— | 1. Do I recopy all of my notes clearly, accurately, and neatly? | ——— |
| ——— | ——— | 2. Do I rework the model problem over and over until I can do it easily? | ——— |
| ——— | ——— | 3. Do I recite explanations of problems aloud as I work, to another or to myself? | ——— |
| ——— | ——— | 4. Do I recheck my computations and my thinking process? | ——— |
| ——— | ——— | 5. Do I test all of my work for reasonableness? | ——— |

# *A P P E N D I X*

# Appendix to Part 4

## *Suggested Reading Questions for SQ3R Step 2 Practice*

The questions that follow are examples; there are no right or wrong answers. The important thing is that your sample questions help you focus on the key points in the text.

### Two possible questions related to Step 1

1. Why is surveying important?

2. How do I survey a chapter?

### Two possible questions related to Step 2

1. How do I create questions from the heading of a section?

2. What words can I use to help me make up questions?

## *Suggested Markings for SQ3R Step 3 Practice*

Compare your underlining and marginal notations with the author's example on the next page. You may have made other markings or used other recall cues. Check: Do your markings highlight the important ideas related to taking care of yourself during stressful study times?

**RECALL CUES**

**Stressful study times happen**

**Stay caught up!**

**Good reasons to take care**

1. **Sleep.**

2. **Avoid stimulants.**

3. **Detachment.**

4. **Physical exercise.**

## ACADEMIC PRESSURE

Of course academic pressure is not applied evenly during the semester or quarter. There are times (especially during midterms and finals) when all your professors will expect special work from you at once. Themes will be due and examinations will be scheduled all within a few days. These demanding periods produce unusual pressure and strain, especially if you have made the mistake of getting behind in your work. The pace picks up, frustrations increase, fear takes a firmer grip, and students appear haggard and drained. It's a period of too much coffee, too many pills, and too little sleep—a desperate time with a touch of madness. Not only does it hurt your physical and mental health, but when the pressures force abnormal behavior, you can make foolish mistakes and jeopardize your academic progress.

How can you keep the peak period madness from hurting you? How can you avoid becoming too tense and frantic? Here are four suggestions: Stick as close as possible to your regular study and work schedule. Avoid late hours. Get some extra work done, but (1) get enough sleep to avoid the tension merry-go-round that spins some students into a state of chaos. (2) Avoid stimulants. Stay away from excessive coffee and drugs that keep you awake but destroy your ability to think clearly and logically when you need to. (3) Assume an air of detachment from the whole crazy rat race. Look at it from a distance. Float through it with a calm head and confident manner. Watch the behavior of others who fall prey to the pressures, but refuse to become over involved yourself. But what if the pressure builds up too much despite your preventive measures? Is there a last-minute safety valve? (4) Physical exercise is a good antidote. (Jog, Play ball, Go bowling.) Physical activity is one way to reduce stress resulting from a heavier-than-usual academic load.

# *Suggested Answers and Markings for SQ3R Step 4 Practice*

1.  Two possible questions related to the text:

    **Question one:** What can you use to help guide you when you recite?

    **Question two:** What is the best way to recite?

Your suggested questions may be somewhat different from these, but see if yours contain the important ideas in the text: a description of Step 4, the information that can help you with this step, how to recite, and the value of recall cues.

Use these same ideas to guide you as you check your work for the rest of the exercise.

2.  Suggested markings and recall cues for the text:

| | |
|---|---|
| **Step 4, Recite** | Once you have formed questions on your reading and have read to answer those questions, you are ready to <u>recite the answers</u>. <u>Use your underlining and markings</u> to guide you. Reciting <u>helps you learn and remember</u> what you have read. Do not skip this step, even if you think you know the information. This step will make a big difference in how well you master the material. |
| **Use markings** | |
| **Always do it!** | |
| **Recite, make notes** | Recite the answers out loud (or quietly to yourself). Also write <u>brief study notes</u>, which will <u>help encode</u> the information in your long-term memory for easier retrieval on the final examination. |
| **Hard? Write summary** | Write a sentence summary of the main idea in each paragraph if the material is extremely difficult for you. |
| **Recall cues save time** | <u>The recall cues you wrote in the margins are an essential step</u>. If you use those cues to recite, you may not need study notes for some classes. |

3.  The following are suggested answers to the questions formulated in the first segment of this exercise. Your answers should go with whatever questions you wrote for that segment.

    **Question one:** What can you use to help guide you when you recite?

    **Suggested answer:** You can use your markings and recall cues as guides for reciting.

    **Question two:** What is the best way to recite?

    **Suggested answer:** Recite out loud if possible (or quietly to yourself).

# Appendix to Part 5

## *Author's Suggested Response to Exercise for Strategy #4*

The numbers increase by 3 each time. You might also have said that this is "counting by three's," or something similar.

## *Author's Suggested Response to Exercise for Strategy #7*

**ROOSTERS:**

> **R**ecite aloud
>
> **O**rganize the material
>
> **O**ver-learn
>
> **S**pread out memory work
>
> **T**est and retest
>
> **E**xpect to remember
>
> **R**ecall with hooks
>
> **S**tudy before sleeping

Did you find another hook for remembering these? Good! The important thing is finding a hook that works for you, not getting one specific "right" word.

# Appendix to Part 6

*Answers to Key Words Matching Quiz*

1. F
2. N
3. K
4. H
5. G
6. I
7. J
8. D
9. M
10. A
11. L
12. E
13. B
14. C

If you are still unsure about the meanings of some of these words, look them up in a dictionary. They are important words in most essay tests and assignments.

*Author's Suggestions for Clustering Exercise*

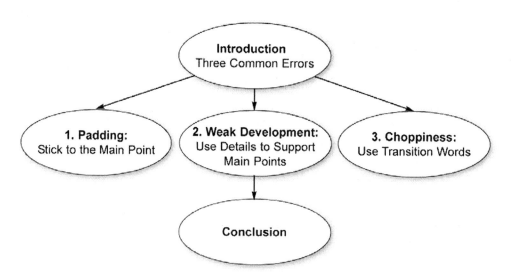

Your clustering may be somewhat different, but it should include in some way the key points noted in this cluster diagram. Notice that this diagram also includes notes for an introduction and a conclusion. Doing this gives you a helpful reminder to include those sections in your essay.

## *Author's Suggestions for Paragraph in Practice with Transition Words*

*An amazing amount of activity goes on in the human brain. There are at least 100 billion nerve cells, or neurons, in your brain. Moreover, each of these neurons is busy making between 5,000 and 50,000 contacts with other neurons! Thus you can consider the brain as a small universe, for it does all this and yet weighs only three pounds.*

Your paragraph may look different. The important thing is that you used the main ideas: the size of the brain compared with the number of neurons and the amount of activity it contains. You also needed to use two transition words somewhere in the paragraph to help connect the ideas.

The transition words used in the sample above are *moreover* and *thus*. Which transition words did you use?

# Appendix to Part 7

*Author's Suggestions for Recall Cues for the Five Rs*

### Recall cues for $R_1$:

Neat clear copy

Can use color

### Recall cues for $R_2$:

Do the model

Over and over!

### Recall cues for $R_3$:

Recite

Explain every step

### Recall cues for $R_4$:

Recheck

Think

Think again!

### Recall cues for $R_5$:

Does it make sense?

You may have used some different recall cues. The important point is to help yourself remember these five important steps for learning math and related subjects.

# Appendix to Part 8

## *Author's Responses for Final Review, Matching Portion*

| Question | Answer | Explanation |
|----------|--------|-------------|
| 1. | B | Review class notes as soon as possible, certainly within 24 hours so that you can clarify abbreviations and garbled notes. |
| 2. | A | Often one of two opposite statements is correct in a multiple-choice question. |
| 3. | Left | Recall cues are placed in the left-hand margin. |
| 4. | D | "None of the above" is correct; the actual answer is 80%. |
| 5. | F | Study time is best broken into intervals of an hour to an hour and a half, with 10-minute breaks. |
| 6. | F | Instead of recopying notes, spend your study time writing study questions and recall phrases and reciting answers out loud. Math notes, however, should be recopied. |
| 7. | F | Visual organizers like trees and maps can be used in any subject. |
| 8. | T | Professional problem solvers think methodically and "talk" themselves through the problem. |
| 9. | T | To avoid too much underlining, read a paragraph first and then underline the important points when you reread it. |
| 10. | F | SQ3R is for reading difficult or complex material. |

Did you get 100% correct? If not, go back into the text to get more information and review the material for those you missed, especially if you scored 70% or less (7 answers or fewer correct).

## *Author's Comments on Final Review, Essay Portion*

Because your essay is about your individual needs and goals, a sample is not included here. But do check the quality of your essay and your action plan using the following questions:

1. Did you start your essay with an introduction that describes what is important to you?

2. Do you have a paragraph on each of the three or four suggestions or ideas that you chose?

3. Did each paragraph give some detail about the suggestion?

4. Did you talk about why the suggestion is important to you?

5. Did you describe how the suggestion will help with your studying?

6. Did you finish with specific details on when and how you will put these suggestions into practice?

# Additional Reading

Andrus, Carol. *Fat-Free Writing.* Crisp Series, 2000.

Banner, James M., and Harold C. Cannon. *The Elements of Learning.* New Haven, CT: Yale University Press, 1999.

Bonet, Diana. *The Business of Listening, Third Edition.* Crisp Series, 2001.

Feldman, Daniel A. *Critical Thinking.* Crisp Series, 2002.

Fry, Ron. *How to Study.* Crisp Series/Delmar, 2005.

————. *Improve Your Reading.* Crisp Series/Delmar, 2005.

Funk, Wilfred, and Norman Lewis. *Thirty Days to a More Powerful Vocabulary.* NY: Pocket Books, 2003.

Haynes, Marion E. *Time Management, Third Edition.* Crisp Series, 2001.

*KAZ® (Keyboarding A-Z): Touch Typing Quick and Easy.* Crisp Series, 2005.

Luckie, William R., Wood Smethurst, and Sara Beth Huntley. *Study Power Workbook.* Brookline, MA: Brookline Books, 2000.

Riley, Lorna. *Achieving Results.* Crisp Series, 2001.

Steinbach, Robert. *Successful Lifelong Learning, Revised Edition.* Crisp Series, 2000.

Whimbey, Arthur, and Jack Lochhead. *Problem Solving and Comprehension, Sixth Edition.* Mahwah, NJ: Lawrence Erlbaum Associates, 1999.